# MODERN CHRISTIANITY,

## A CIVILIZED HEATHENISM.

BY THE AUTHOR OF

"THE FIGHT AT DAME EUROPA'S SCHOOL."

BOSTON:

WILLIAM F. GILL AND COMPANY,

SUCCESSORS TO THE OLD STAND OF SHEPARD AND GILL,

151 WASHINGTON STREET.

1875.

STEREOTYPED BY
C. J. PETERS & SON, 73 FEDERAL STREET, BOSTON.

PRESS OF RAND, AVERY, & CO., BOSTON.

# PREFACE.

THE question which is beginning to agitate the religious world is not whether we shall continue to recite damnatory clauses in our Athanasian Creed, but whether there is any creed whatever that is worth reciting; not whether this form of Christianity is preferable to that, but whether all forms of Christianity pretending to come from God through Christ are not gross impositions from beginning to end. No man who reads a newspaper, or listens to a conversation in his common room or at his club, will consent to place the impending controversy on any narrower basis. Revealed religion is on its trial before the world, not for some trifling blemishes which a little mild correction may mend, but for its very life; and if the clergy, its natural defenders, can show no intelligible reason why it should stand, common-sense, in this country at least, will very speedily decide upon its merits, after a somewhat rough-and-ready fashion.

Christianity is one of two things; and the whole matter before us resolves itself into the question, which of these two things it is. It is a human philosophy, founded by a great moral teacher called Christ, who was so much better than Epicurus or Zeno, inasmuch as he hit upon a system which was better adapted for civilizing the world, and taught precepts nobler, purer, more disinterested, more unselfish, than the precepts of any other school: or it is a distinct revelation of God's will, brought down from heaven by Christ the only-begotten Son; claiming not to improve upon human philosophies, but to supersede them, to upset them, to annihilate them; establishing in their stead a kingdom mysterious, supernatural, unearthly, opposed in every sense to the traditions of this lower world. Christianity is one of these two things; but it cannot be both of them together. If it be a very excellent philosophy, it is not essentially divine, because man could have found out such a philosophy for himself; unless, indeed, you are content to accept God merely as the indefinite source of every upright principle in the human mind. But, if it be essentially divine, it is not a very excellent philosophy, because it forces man into the highly unphilosophic attitude of holding all things around him in utter contempt, in order that he may win a heaven so thoroughly opposed to earth, that the one has to be finally burnt up before the other can be opened. It is not a very excellent philosophy, because it threatens man with a hell whose tortures are so unspeakably horrible, that, unless you suppose his nature to be so far changed as to make him regard pain as a pleasurable sensation, every muscle of his hand and foot must be paralyzed with fear whenever he contemplates his possible doom. It is not a very excellent philosophy, because it demands the constant imitation, in every word and deed, of a Christ who never opened his mouth without furiously enraging all the philosophers of the day; and who made himself either a laughing-stock, or an object of absolute detestation, to every creature with whom he came in contact, excepting those for whose benefit he was working miracles, or performing acts of superhuman love, — acts as contrary to every philosophic principle as light is contrary to darkness. It is not a very excellent philosophy, because, in the Catholic Church at least, it prescribes a form of worship which either involves the most absurd superstition that ever amused the philosophic mind, or commits the faithful worshipper to an enthusiasm of devotion so intense, to a penitence so abject, to vows of amendment so solemn, that his whole life, if he pretends to live out his prayers, must needs be passed in the defiance of every philosophic theory, and in the atmosphere of another world. Clearly enough, if Christianity is the best means of civilizing mankind, it did not come from God; and, if it came from God through Christ, it is of all the methods most unlikely to promote the civilization of mankind.

Now, the weak point about our present system of religion, the origin of all those doubts and difficulties and contradictions and uncertainties, which tend to universal unbelief as surely as cause produces effect, appears to me to be just precisely this, that whereas Christianity must either be a human philosophy, designed to make this earth a pleasanter place to live in, or else a message from God, bidding men make this earth as unpleasant to themselves as possible, so as to secure hereafter the joys of heaven, — our weak point appears to be, that, whereas Christianity can only be one of these two things, we modern Christians have made up our minds that Christianity shall be to us both the one thing and the other. And we shall never heal our divisions and distractions, or gain any real influence over the world, or cease to provoke the contemptuous smile, or to enjoy the well-bred forbearance, of reasonable men, until our archbishops and bishops, or our two houses of convocation, or whatever other voice may be supposed to ha e authority among us, shall plainly declare which of these two things Christianity is. If it be only a human philosophy, then we shall know what we are about. A national religion is a very wholesome thing. People have always set up some sort of superstition; and Christianity is probably a better kind of superstition than any other. All religions, too, have had their heroic ages and their myths, their ritual and their ceremonial, their promises and their threats; and there can be no reason why our modern religion should be denied its rightful share. But if Christianity be what it pretends to be, the divinely-appointed channel for saving, throughout all eternity, the souls of men, then we are instantly brought face to face with four tremendous facts, any one of which is sufficient by itself to determine, with unhesitating exactness, what our mode of life must be. These facts are, (1) the duty of imitating Christ, (2) the prayer-book standard of devotion, (3) the difficulty of gaining heaven, (4) the everlasting flames of hell; and, until we consent to alter the documents wherein these four facts stand inscribed, we cannot escape their logical consequences, theorize as we may.

We have to imitate Christ; and there cannot exist two opinions as to the sort of life which he is represented to have led. The one characteristic feature of his conduct — the one point which separated him from the philosophers who had gone before, and made him distinctively Christ — was his opposition to the world. It was not merely that he preached an unpopular austerity. This had been done before; and the openly vicious and luxurious had relished such preaching as little from the lips of Socrates as from the lips of Christ. The point at which philosophy stopped short (because it was of earth), and Christ began (because he was from heaven), was in the attack not on vice, but on virtue. He taught that the *righteousness* of men, not their wickedness, was as filthy rags; that the sternest type of morality was worthless before God, unless sanctified by faith, and beautified by graces sought of him in prayer. He taught the submission of the entire heart and conscience to his Spirit, as to a personal, ever-present guide, without whose co-operation deeds might be fair and motives honorable, but the inner life would yet be lived at enmity with God. He taught thus; and so men hated him, not as they hated the philosopher, who had quarrelled with their sensual, grovelling pleasures, but as they could only hate One who threw their very goodness in their teeth, and convicted them of blindness in the very things wherein they thought their vision was so clear. And so they hated him; and if there is one syllable of truth in the Bible, from Genesis to the Revelation, this truth stands out as the leading text of every page, — that, for the selfsame reason for which these men hated Christ, their fathers had hated God ever since his prophets first revealed him, and their sons would go on hating him till the end of time; would hate him as they hate him even now, because he interferes not with the passions which they know already to be bad and evil, but with the standard it has pleased them to set up of the lawful and the good. A man does not need any Christ to tell him when he has debased himself to the level of the beast. His country punishes him for open notorious crime; his very excesses are themselves the avengers of his darling sin; and society has, for the most part, a sterner sentence to pass upon special forms of guilt than either conscience or penal code. It is the office of Christ — the one precise office which makes him Christ, and divides him from all the moralists that ever went before him — to convict the respectable, upright, good-natured, courteous gentleman, from the first beginning of Christian centuries in Jerusalem down to the last century that shall ever be; to convict such a man of idolatry and stubbornness of heart, because he is being daily conformed to this world, instead of being transformed into the likeness of God. If Christ is any thing better than a human teacher of self-consistent truths, it is at this point that his business with men begins. For this they hate him; and, as they hate him, so has he declared that they will hate all those who belong to him. Until the world is wholly converted, which nobody yet pretends, his people must ever wage with it a deadly war. There can be no peace between two such armies as the soldiers of Christ and the servants of the Devil. His disciples must fight as their Captain fought, making themselves an offence, a nuisance, an abhorrence, to every man who is not, like them, an open confessor of his name. This is the one test, the only test, by which our Christian faithfulness is to be tried. Any hypocrite can prate about his faith and his feelings. The Christian is to take up a manful position at the point where he stands most in need of all his strength and courage; and there, openly before client and friend and patron, there, just where the struggle is hardest, is to suffer and dare. Here is the one proof of true membership with Christ; for in this world, at least, we can give no other. I refrain, however strongly tempted, from quoting texts, — partly because a string of quotations makes a very unreadable book; partly because I should never know where to stop, for the whole New Testament might be cited; partly because I am unwilling to mix up with writings which may probably be misunderstood any words or allusions which all men cherish as sacred. But I challenge the reader of any Gospel or Epistle in the Scriptures to produce one single page which does not more or less distinctly set forth the truth, that to be hated and persecuted and ridiculed from morning till night, by all the world, is in all ages, ancient and modern alike, the eternal, immutable, unfailing test of the Christianity that comes from Christ. Hold any theory you please about the extent to which he went into society, and say, if you dare, that he dined with publicans and sinners because he liked their company, and relished their good cheer, and the fact will yet remain, that his life was one incessant declaration of war, — not against the grosser forms of secret or open sin; for to these, on the other hand, he was ever most merciful, — but against the common-sense of the clever man of the world, and the godlessness of public opinion. Make what allowance you please for weaknesses of the flesh, and unavoidable inconsistencies, on the part of those who would copy an example so far above their reach, you cannot possibly deny that Christ has made his life the exact pattern of our life, — a pattern not to be looked at from a distance with calm approval, but to be imitated with painful efforts which must never tire, — a pattern which we can only follow so long as our attitude is one of vigorous assault on every evil thing we see before us, — a pattern which we have infallibly declined, if we are so much as on speaking terms with the enemies of our Lord. If Christ's example be any thing to us at all, we Christians have no business even to stand willingly in the presence of an ungodly man, unless we are feeding him, or converting him, or doing him some bodily or spiritual good.

The plain truth is, that our Christian beliefs are immeasurably *too big* for any standard of Christian practice which common-sense permits us to follow; and when we find ourselves in this dilemma, instead of confessing that we have made some terrible mistake, and that our beliefs are either all wrong, or our actions indefensible, we are dishonest enough to argue backwards, to make up our minds what sort of life it will be sensible and sociable and convenient to lead, and then to pretend that our beliefs were meant to be qualified in order to agree with our predetermined line of conduct. We admit, for instance, that it is our duty to imitate Christ, and that the one characteristic feature of his life was his state of incessant enmity against the world. We find it inconvenient, however, thus to proclaim our religion wherever we go, to be marked men in every circle wherein we move, to expose ourselves to hatred, persecution, and ridicule, whenever we come in contact with our neighbors; and so we calmly assume that times are changed, and that whereas it was, no doubt, the Christian's duty in the earlier centuries of the faith to fight manfully in his Master's name, and openly to publish his belief, at the risk even of bonds and martyrdom, it has become the Christian's duty, in these later days, to avoid every kind of singularity, to do very much as others do, and by all means to keep his religion smuggled up in his own heart, lest the wicked world should laugh at him. In short, finding that Christianity is opposed to common-sense (which Christ, if he was Christ at all, must expressly have intended it to be), and being forced to make definite choice between the one principle and the other, we accept common-sense — the philosophy of civilized heathenism — as the guide of our daily life, and keep Christianity for our acts of devotion, for periods of solemnity or sentiment, and for times when we think we are going to die. This is somewhere about what the modern Christian's imitation of Christ is worth; and I ask any honest man to say whether such a contradiction between faith and practice is, or is not, a barefaced, transparent absurdity.

No less apparent must it be that the second of our four great facts — the prayer-book standard of devotion — is utterly incompatible with any other life than the literal painful struggling imitation of Christ, action for action, word for word. Here, again, I forbear to quote; but every psalm and every collect supports my view. If the strong crying wherewith we seek to move our God to pity, if the grateful thanks we render him for his abundant love, if either prayers or praises in church on Sunday, have any sense at all, they positively forbid our spending the week in money-making, or worldly pleasure, or any other work than that of anxious preparation for judgment, and acts of mercy towards Christ's poor. And if it be thought that even yet there is room for cavilling, that my argument proves too much, and that the example of Christ is absurdly beyond our efforts, and the prayer-book standard of devotion obviously intended to set us aiming at a great deal, in the hope that we may reach, at any rate, a very little; if this be urged, then what shall we say of the other two tremendous facts, — of heaven and hell? Are they, also, to be "qualified," or explained away? Grant, if you please, that Christ's example was meant only to be admired, and that our psalms and litanies have no loftier practical design than to put us periodically into a devotional frame of mind. How are you going to deal with the very substantial truth (if it be a truth at all) that forever and forever each one of us is to dwell amid the inconceivable delights of heaven, or the appalling agonies of hell? Have these familiar pictures, too, been over-colored by our spiritual guides, to serve the very immoral purpose of tempting us into morality by telling us lies? Or if they be really truths, and such truths as to place every thing but themselves absolutely out of sight, what can any reasonable man among us care to do, when he has provided food and clothing just sufficient to keep his own family alive, but spend the entire residue of his worldly goods in ministering to the poor and sorrowing, and the entire residue of his time in praising Christ his Saviour for the blessed hope of heaven, or in tearful supplication for deliverance from the terrors of hell? If it were not a question of obvious duty, the common instinct of self-preservation would be enough to decide the matter. No man with one grain of sense, if he soberly believed that he was to live upon this earth for threescore years and ten, and then to live in heaven or hell for threescore million centuries ten times told, would consent to spend one short minute of his life in any work which did not tangibly and obviously tend to make his salvation more secure. If this should be denied, and it should be urged that the mind of man is constituted with a view to present action, and is incapable of brooding over possible futurities, I would ask, Who constituted it thus? Has God, who is represented as all-merciful, and as longing to save our souls, has he threatened us with everlasting torment, if we do not obey his will, and at the same time so created us as to make it impossible for us to be very much afraid of his judgments? Has he said to us poor, miserable creatures, "I shall damn you to all eternity, if you do not consecrate your whole life and being to my service; but if you dare to be overwhelmed with terror at such a thought, and to go about weeping, and wringing your hands, and crying to me for salvation, I shall say that you are neglecting your worldly duties, and shall damn you all the more"? This, if you come to look the matter fairly in the face, is what the modern Christian tries to make himself believe that God has said, when he pretends that God has threatened him with eternal flames, and yet has enjoined upon him the duty of being merry and glad. Only on the supposition that the Christian's life is to be a facsimile of Christ's, and that he who does not follow him painfully step by step is crucifying him over again; only thus is it possible for an intelligent being to believe that any man can deserve to be forever burnt alive. If it be true that the human mind cannot realize the horrors that await the impenitent, such a constitution was never ordained by a merciful God, but by a crafty Devil. It can only be a device to lull the perishing millions into false security. And, if so, the very existence of such a device strengthens my argument a hundred-fold. For what are the clergy doing? What are the benevolent religious laity doing? What are our Christian women doing? They stand before God, responsible, each one according to his gifts, for the salvation of a world which neither loves nor fears him. They believe not only that the enormous majority of themselves and others will be burnt alive forever, unless the uncovenanted mercy of God steps in specially to save them, but also that the Devil has been so subtle as almost to cut off man's last chance of safety, by preventing him from realizing that being burnt alive is a very dreadful thing. And yet, with this responsibility and this belief, they laugh and sing, and dance and play, and make merry after every conceivable fashion which their tastes suggest, and their means afford. Christian women drive and dress; and Christian men hunt and dine; and Christian children, who may die to-morrow, are told to enjoy themselves while they can; and Christian priests and Christian bishops join the happy throng, and say that it is all right and proper, and laugh with the loudest, and joke with the funniest, and would think it the very worst possible taste, if some wicked unbeliever were humbly to suggest a doubt whether any gentleman or lady present had one single thought in common with the persecuted, despised, and sorrowing Christ. This is what orthodox Christians do. And when the simple-minded Briton wonders much within himself how they can reconcile such lives with damnatory clauses, and the abject poverty of Christ, and dares to ask some wise philosopher among them to explain, the wise philosopher falls upon him straightway, and crushes him then and there, and tells him that he is an infidel, and an atheist, and a free-thinker, and a sceptic, and laughs to scorn his ignorance in presuming to suppose, that because Christ was poor, and bade his followers be like him, there is any thing in the world to prevent a Christian bishop from taking rank among dukes and earls, and enjoying an income of fifteen thousand pounds a year; or that the fact that each one of us stands in peril of torments that shall never cease is any reason whatever why we should not thoroughly enjoy ourselves until the day of torment comes.

The few weeks lately passed have witnessed a spectacle sufficiently instructive, in the judgment of an ordinarily constituted mind, to fix the value of ecclesiastical anathemas forever. The flower — perhaps, rather, the ripe fruit — of our English clergy, the richest, luckiest, and portliest of our country rectors, as well as the most dignified ornaments of our cathedral stalls, have journeyed pleasantly up to town to discuss with wonted clerical vigor, and something less than clerical concern, whether or no it is to be "believed faithfully" that a vast majority of God's creatures will be tortured in everlasting flames. How these gentlemen occupied themselves, when released each day from the excitement of debate, we are not informed; but those who know the clergy best are best aware that there are less agreeable ways of spending the inside of a week than accompanying a clerical friend to London, and that such visits, for the most part, are by no means to be accurately described as painful pilgrimages to a shrine. We do know, however, to what extent the members of convocation maintained their impressive composure during the debate itself; and we never read that any canon or archdeacon, however warm he may have waxed on his own account in sparring with his reverend brother, so far forgot the manners of a polished gentleman as to break down utterly, out of simple kindliness of heart, while he professed his awful belief that millions upon millions of his fellow-countrymen would be eternally burnt alive. With what appetite our dignitaries attacked their dinner in the evening, and what their dinner cost, and how peacefully they slept at night, are questions far too practical to be orthodox,—questions, indeed, which none but a flippant infidel would have the bad taste to raise. It shall be left for other than flippant infidels to answer, at their leisure, a question yet more practical, and say how beings fashioned out of common flesh and blood, with human sympathies and human ties, with wives and daughters to make their firesides bright at home, and happy boys leading happy romping lives, and running every conceivable mad-English risk at school, can talk the theology of the orthodox Anglican divine, and ever care to eat or drink, or fall willingly asleep again.

That Christianity, as the professed religion of English men and women, will survive the scrutinies of the next fifty or eighty years, is more than I may dare to say. But this much I will say, that, if it does survive, it will survive on the principles which I have tried to sketch out at the close of the following little dialogue, and on no other principles whatever. Its present position before the world is hopelessly untenable, and would not be tolerated for a single day, did it not manifestly suit the world's purpose to extend its gracious forbearance yet a little longer towards so valuable an ally. Nay, as I have been taunted with unfaithfulness for daring to submit that solemn beliefs ought to be either acted out, or else abjured, I may be permitted to add, that our modern Christianity will never be defended by any man who is not personally interested in the perpetuation of a contemptible unreality, or who does not, for some higher reason, judge it prudent to deprecate inquiry into a system which will not bear the light of day. If public opinion (by which I mean, not the so-called rationalists who *write*, but the so-called Christians, also, who approvingly *read*),— if public opinion cared to speak its mind, public opinion would proclaim itself infidel to the very core, — infidel, not by any means as denying the extreme respectability of a good old-fashioned conservative reverence for the Bible and the Church, — infidel, not as feeling disposed to contemplate without horror and alarm the bold avowal of atheistic tendencies in the popular mind, — infidel, not as being blind to the historical fact that nations without creeds and pious traditions have become reckless and revolutionary, and abandoned to disorder and misrule, — but infidel, as flatly disbelieving that Christ, the very and eternal God, did visibly live on this material earth the life of poverty and pain and sorrow, which every one of us Christians ought to be living now; that he did visibly stretch his arms upon the cross, that we might crucify ourselves with him at every instant of every day; that he did visibly mount up to heaven to make ready a place therein for those who are brave enough to live as he lived, and die as he died; that he will visibly come again to call us trembling creatures to account for every word we speak, and every act we do; that he will cast into flames intolerable, that shall never, never be quenched, each one of us living men and women who has been afraid to confess him boldly before all the world. This is what public opinion disbelieves, and what the Catholic Church proclaims. This, and nothing short of this, is the Christianity of Christ. It is either false, or it is true. If it be false, the sooner we alter our Christian documents, and leave off threatening men with judgments which will never overtake them, the better. If it be true, I confess myself wholly unable to understand how any man who seriously believes it, and who contemplates the horrible destiny of those millions of living ones who deny or ignore its truth, can ever cease from weeping, or ever rise from his knees, unless it be that he may go forth straightway, and implore his sinful brother, for whom Christ died, to escape, while yet escape is possible, from the yawning gulf of hell.

MARCH, 1873.

# MODERN CHRISTIANITY, Etc.

---

Towards the close of this year's long vacation, I received a visit from an infidel friend; or rather, as I should perhaps say, from a friend who is a genuine heathen, but a naturalized Englishman. His grandfather, Sir Jamjeebhoy Curtsetjee, who received a baronetcy as a reward for having amassed an enormous fortune by opium-smuggling, was, no doubt, a rigorous Parsee; but my friend appears to have found the ancient tenets of his faith somewhat inconvenient, and to have gradually drifted into believing in nothing whatever. I should not, on that account, style him as a "heathen of the worst class:" at any rate, if such be his unhappy state, he contrives so successfully to conceal his degradation as to pass among his fellows at Lincoln's Inn for as good a Christian as most other people. Though thoroughly well acquainted with the religious controversies of the day, he is not fond, as a general rule, of talking about them; and probably nobody, excepting myself and half a dozen equally intimate friends, has any idea that he is a heathen at all. To this short sketch of his natural history, I will only add, that being a younger brother, and in no danger of succession to the family honors, he has had the good sense to abbreviate his name to Curtis; that he has read, with considerable diligence, the Bible and other Christian books; and that he is distinguished, even among members of his own learned profession, for the remarkable vigor and acuteness of his mind.

As for me, I hold a small town-living in the south of England, — small, that is, in point of income, but a good deal larger than I like as regards population. However, I "keep" a curate, who shares my work; and, both of us being bachelors, we get on very well together. I congratulate myself the rather on this point, because my married friend Jones, who holds an adjacent rectory, can never by any chance keep a curate for six weeks at a time. If the poor young man be single, Mrs. Jones sits upon him to that extent, that the place becomes unendurable; and, if he be married, the two wives grow so frightfully jealous of one another's influence in the parish, that it is more than the two husbands can do to keep the peace between them.

On the whole, I am pretty comfortably off. I have good health, kind neighbors, and work which suits me. I do not know what a man can wish besides. I can drive my friends from the station in my own trap, and give them a very fair bottle of claret after dinner. It was on this wise that I entertained my heathen guest some weeks ago; and, when we had drunk as much wine as was good for us, we made ourselves very particularly snug in my study, over a couple of long clay pipes and a small September fire.

"I see that your archbishop has been pitching into us," observed Curtis, throwing down "The Times."

"Upon my word," answered I, "it seems to me that you are all making a great fuss about nothing! It is hard lines indeed, that a man can't say a few commonplace words on an exceedingly commonplace subject, but they must be telegraphed all over the universe, as if he were a lawgiver."

"Oh! pray don't suppose that I am going to quarrel with him," rejoined my friend. "From his point of view, he is quite right to say that we are in a state of darkness, and need conversion. Only, if he, or any one else who holds with him, imagines that he is at all likely to convert us, he labors under a very painful delusion."

"And why?"

"Simply because we should scarcely think it worth while to make so very insignificant a change. We are all pretty much as he is already. Tell me, my dear fellow: what should I have to give up, if I turned Christian to-morrow?"

"Give up? Oh! why—let me see. Oh! you would have to give up lots of things."

"Well, let us have one thing at a time."

"Oh! of course: you would have to give up—let me see. You don't drink, do you?"

"About as much as you do, that is all."

"Nor swear?"

"No, indeed! I think the habit extremely weak and snobbish."

"And I suppose your life in London, taking it altogether, is tolerably correct?"

"Every bit as correct as your own."

"Ah, well! you are an unusually good specimen, you see. Upon my word, old fellow, I don't know what you would have to give up, exactly."

"No, I see you don't. But Christ would have known. If I had put the question to him, he would have told me to give up all that I had in the world, — to fling it, as if it were dung, at the foot of his cross, — and then to follow him."

"Oh, yes! of course," said I, knocking the ashes out of my pipe, and reaching out my hand for the pouch, preparatory to lighting up again. "Oh, yes! of course. If you put it in that way, I see what you mean."

"I do put it in that way. That is the way, as far as I understand, in which every question touching Christianity *must* be put. Now, look here, old fellow. You won't be offended if I speak my mind. I am a heathen; and I don't believe in Christ one bit. I think the whole story of his coming to this earth in the highest degree improbable, — so improbable, that only one sort of evidence would induce me to accept it as a fact. That sort of evidence I do not find to be forthcoming; and therefore I reject the entire narrative as mythical and absurd."

"And, pray, what sort of evidence is it which would convince you?"

"The steadfast, personal witness to Christ, of those who profess to believe in him. I myself deny that any such person ever lived; but, supposing he did live, there can be no question whatever what he said and did, and commanded his disciples to say and do; for, however difficult the interpretation of your Bible may sometimes be with regard to doctrine, in the matter of practical conduct it is absolutely consistent from beginning to end. The text of the entire New Testament enjoins one leading principle, which no child can misunderstand; and that principle is the downright literal renunciation of this present world. Every species of self-indulgence is declared to be sinful. The Christian is to permit himself no kind of pleasure, but the pleasure which comes to him out of communion with Christ. At every point, in season and out of season, he is to fight with all his strength against the spirit of worldliness; and, lest there should arise any mistake about terms, worldliness is over and over again defined, with palpable clearness, to be every thing and any thing outside Christ. Without immediate reference to Christ, as to a personal guide standing ever by, no action is to be performed, no word spoken, no thought conceived. This is the sort of life which the founder of Christianity has bidden his disciples lead. Will you kindly tell me how many of them lead it?"

"My dear fellow, you expect impossibilities. We are but human; and no man on earth could lead the life which you describe."

"Then Christ has commanded what is contradictory and absurd, and Christianity becomes ridiculous; which is precisely my own opinion.

I don't know who made this earth, and I don't care; but the very fact that it is fair and winning seems to me to justify men in thoroughly enjoying themselves while they live in it. But, if I were a Christian, I should not think so; for Christ has explained in the simplest terms this very mystery. He says, 'You shall take your choice. This world is filled with allurements and delights in order that your strength of purpose may be tried. If you like to enjoy the good things which it has to offer, enjoy them, and lose your reward hereafter: but if, for love towards me, you are content to sacrifice all that gives you pleasure on earth, and to follow, step by step, my pure and self-denying life, you shall have tribulation here; but joy, such as never entered into the heart of man, shall be your portion in heaven.' Now, you Christians appear to think that you can have as much of this world's pleasure as you care to have, and secure the pleasures of the world to come besides."

"We don't think any thing of the kind," said I; "but you can't expect our faith and practice to be everywhere and always consistent."

"No; I expect nothing half so unreasonable. But my charge against you is not that you are inconsistent, and that you fall, through weakness of the flesh, far short of the standard set for your imitation, but that you claim it is a right, and uphold it as a duty, to mix just as freely with the world as if you were heathens. In this matter the modern Christian, with consummate impudence, flatly gives the lie to every precept of his Master. Christ says, 'Renounce the world. Come out of it. Have nothing to do with it. It is utterly opposed to me; and, if you would be my disciple, you must take care that it be utterly opposed to you.' The modern Christian says, 'I shall do nothing of the kind. On the contrary, I conceive it to be my special business to remain in the world, to do very much as other people do, and to show all men how possible it is to serve God, and conform to the usages of society, as well.' Christ says, 'Strip yourself of your wealth. Give it up to me, — all, all of it, — and make yourself poor, that I may enrich you with treasures in heaven.' The modern Christian says, 'No. I don't believe that any such tremendous sacrifice is required of me. The good things of this world were bestowed upon us that we might enjoy them; and so long as I am moderately charitable in my gifts, and refrain from indulging to excess, there can be no reason why I should not keep my money.' Christ says, 'When thou makest a feast, call the poor.' The modern Christian says, 'By no means. I shall do nothing so absurd. The duties of my station require me to keep up my social rank, and to dine only with my friends and equals.' Christ says"—

"Well," interrupted I rather angrily, "you need not say any more. I could say it all for you. Of course, if once you come to talk like that, you can condemn us and our conventionalities at every point. But how is it possible that we can act otherwise? If everybody did literally as Christ has bidden him, the world could not go on."

"Precisely so. And that is the reason why I disbelieve in your religion; because it reduces all things to an absurdity. But *you* have no right to think that it does so. Surely, you are bound, as a man of honor, to accept Christ, absurdities and all; or else to reject him altogether. No doubt, the world could not go on. But did it never occur to you, my friend, that Christ, if he came on earth at all, must have come for the very purpose of preventing the world from going on? He found it going on, going on fast enough, and something to spare. He came expressly to stop it. He came to defeat its progress and prosperity, and to subdue its kingdoms to himself. What are the maxims of political economy to Christ? What are the intricacies of commercial business to Christ? What are the customs of polite society to Christ? He wants your life, and the life of every creature for whom you say he died, to be given up without reserve to him. He wants your churches to be thronged with faithful worshippers, singing his praises all day long. He wants your homes to be pure and lovely, bright with the virtues which your children have copied direct from him. The world could not go on, indeed! No: if Christians lived as

Christ has bidden them, they would create a revolution; and a revolution would be inconvenient. Therefore Christians very wisely determine to drift along quietly with the world, and let well alone."

"I think you are nara upon us, Curtis; I do, indeed. You must admit that Christianity has wrought a great change. See how much purer and better the world is than it was when Christ came."

"Is it? I very much doubt the fact. Of course, people are more civilized than they were eighteen hundred years ago. But Christ need not have come upon this earth to civilize it. Time, and the natural development of the human mind, would have done that. Or, if you think that time alone would not have done it, at any rate, it would have been sufficient that some philosopher — some very good man, and nothing more — should give mankind the benefit of his teaching. If Christ be all that you say he is, you will scarcely put forward the state of social or public life in this country, or in any other, as a satisfactory result of his work and mission."

"No, indeed! He came to save souls."

"To save those only who would lose their life on earth for his sake. My dear fellow, you are in a desperate difficulty. You are defending an illogical position; and such positions refuse to be defended. Christ says distinctly, that you cannot serve God and mammon; and you Christians, with one consent, have steadily resolved that that is precisely the thing which you will do. You are serving God and mammon every day. And you do so, not by reason of inconsistencies, which would be pardonable enough, but as a matter of deliberate purpose, because you believe it to be your privilege or your duty. And, as far as I can judge, you good folks who call yourselves High Churchmen are the worst offenders of all. The old Evangelicals, who led the religious revival fifty or sixty years ago, although so one-sided in doctrine as to alienate all men with Church tendencies, were far more nearly right in their ideas about Christian practice. Their preachers did, at any rate, denounce with bravery every kind of worldliness, and warn men that the whole heart, and not a certain part of it, must be yielded up to Christ. But when they collapsed for want of churchmanship, and the Tractarians took their place, straightway, as if out of pure perversity and spite, these last permitted their disciples to indulge in an almost unlimited amount of secularity. Because the Simeonites had said that balls and operas were sinful, the Puseyites must needs maintain that it was almost a duty, among people of a certain rank in life, to patronize both the one and the other. And so, when the Belgravian fine lady, who has been lounging and frittering away her morning after a fashion of which any intelligent heathen would be ashamed, bids her coachman set her down at All Saints, Margaret Street, at five o'clock, where she pays, with many crossings and bowings, what she is pleased to call her evening devotions to an almost unknown God, instead of being rebuked for her hypocrisy, she is very much applauded for her churchmanship, and is told that such a jumbling together of temporal and spiritual avocations is quite the correct thing. Indeed, the sight of such a woman inside a church is enough to condemn your entire religious system. Look at her, whether she be Belgravian fine lady, or wife of the moderately affluent parson, or an example drawn from any conceivable class between the two. Look at her, with her bracelets, her diamonds, her pearls; look at her dress, the very materials of which would buy coals enough to keep ten old women warm throughout the winter. Why does not the parson tell her to strip herself of her ghastly ornaments, and give to the poor? Would Christ have tolerated such a woman in his presence for a single instant, without administering such a rebuke as would have rung in her ears till her dying-day? Look at her at home, with her lazy habits, and her profitless pursuits, and her silly conversation. Look at her drawing-room, with its costly mirrors, its luxurious sofas, its drapery, and its gilding. Christian, indeed! Why, you must know perfectly well that Christ could not sit in such a room, could not stand in it, could not so much as look in at the doorway, without condemning the monstrous iniquity of such wholesale waste and self-indulgence. Will the parson look in at the doorway too, and tell her this? Not he. It would not be good taste, forsooth; and I should not be surprised if her ladyship were to say that he was no gentleman."

"My dear friend," said I, "you are talking a vast amount of nonsense. How could I possibly tell a lady to strip off her jewels, and give them to the poor? The people would all think me mad, and I should lose half my influence in the parish for ever and ever. And, as for drawing-room luxuries, you must understand that Christianity does not pretend to lay down laws about the furnishing of private houses. People must live according to their means. Besides, you are most unjust and most uncharitable. I dare say that the sort of woman you are describing is an excellent wife and mother, doing her duty in the state of life to which she has been called, generous to the poor, good-natured to her friends, and full of kindly feelings and liberal deeds. There are dozens of such persons in my own parish; and it would be an uncommonly good thing for society in general, if there were dozens more. I am sure we cannot afford to run such people down."

"I don't run them down at all. I am perfectly satisfied with them. The thing which does not satisfy me is, that you should have the assurance to claim such people as Christians. They are not Christians at all. They are civilized heathens. Heathen is not a bad word. It does not mean cannibal. It simply means one who does not believe in God; and a man may decline to believe in God, and yet may talk and act like a decent member of society. You Christians have contrived to make the word offensive by quietly appropriating all virtue and goodness to yourselves, and speaking of us poor heathen with a pious shudder, as if we were in a helpless state of darkness and ferocity. We thank you kindly for your compassion; but we beg to say that we are accustomed to meet in society, every day of our lives, dozens of men, and dozens of women too, who never say a prayer, and dozens more, calling themselves Christians, who pray after such a fashion, that they might just as well save themselves the trouble. We meet, I say, continually, dozens of men and women living utterly without God, heathen from head to foot, who would not do a mean or immoral or unkind action, and would not willingly say one syllable which could distress a friend, for any consideration in the world."

"Then I say that such persons, whatever their religious professions may be, are practically Christians."

"I say that they are nothing of the kind. They disbelieve in Christ entirely, and, as a necessary consequence, disbelieve in heaven and hell. Whatever virtues they exhibit in their lives are heathen virtues, common to all civilized humanity. They are in no sense indebted to Christ for the instinct which prompts them to be good-natured and straightforward. It suits the purpose of you Christians to pretend that all such virtues are graces bestowed in answer to prayer; but I tell you that men who never pray, and never have prayed, possess the highest and best of virtues in abundance, and practise them continually. What!

is there no good-nature, no kindliness of heart, no generous impulse, excepting among those who profess your creed? Am I a savage, because I do not believe in Christ? Were the ancient Greeks and Romans bloodthirsty and brutal, and devoid of all natural affection and honor? You, if you have ever read any classics, must know that they were nothing of the kind. I make bold to say that there does not exist one essential point of difference between the fine lady of Grosvenor Square and the fine lady of Athens or of Rome, except this only, — that whereas the one, towards the close of each day's frivolity, pays her devotions at St. Paul's, Knightsbridge, or All Saints, the other performed a similar act of worship at the temple of her god. Of course, in numberless little points of culture, the modern lady will be found to surpass the ancient; but this is a matter of civilization, and has nothing whatever to do with Christianity."

"I beg your pardon. It has every thing to do with Christianity."

"Then, as I said before, you claim, as the

result of Christ's mission upon earth, that, after eighteen centuries of gospel preaching, he has made the fine lady of Christian England a trifle more good-natured than the fine lady of heathen Greece. Truly, a most glorious triumph! No, no, my friend. If God ever humbled himself to be born of a woman, it was to make some greater difference in woman's life than this. It was that he might drag the fine lady from her carriage and her boudoir, and clothe her in homely garments, and plant her by the bedside of the sick and dying, — plant her there, not as a casual visitor, condescending to stoop from her greatness just once in a way, but plant her there, and bid her live and grow there, making it her adopted dwelling-place, where she might brighten with her simple goodness the abode of poverty, and perhaps of sin."

"But, my dear Curtis, many of our women already do this sort of work, and do it admirably well."

"I am not speaking of those who do it, but of those who don't. Will you maintain that a hundredth part of those who might do it are thus engaged? And have you the courage, under your present refined system of religious teaching, have you the courage to tell one fine lady to her face, as you hand her down to dinner, that this is the work to which her life should be devoted?"

"Yes, I think I could dare to tell her so, if I thought it wise. But I should not think it wise, by any means. You appear to me to misunderstand entirely the object of Christianity, and the essential conditions of a Christian life. Christ never intended to make us all monks and sisters of mercy. What a very stupid, humdrum world this would be, with nothing but hermits in it!"

"And what a very stupid, humdrum place heaven must be, with nothing but saints and angels in it!"

"Don't interrupt me, old fellow. You really must be practical. My idea is, that Christ came to make men good citizens, useful members of society, kind neighbors, conscientious doers of such work as their several stations in life require. He came to teach us great principles, and lofty motives of action, to shed the love of God in our hearts, and to sanctify our homes. If, therefore, a man performs his business diligently, speaks the truth, says his prayers, and gives what he can spare to the poor, I call him a good Christian; and I say that he is doing all that Christ expects of him. Some, no doubt, are called to higher deeds than others. Some are bidden to make painful sacrifices, and noble efforts of self-denial. But the ordinary Christian may be content if he earns his living honestly, believes in Christ faithfully, and resists the Devil manfully."

"In short, he may be content if he attains the level of a highly cultivated heathen. I quite agree with you. That is precisely the level which I trust that I have attained myself; and it satisfies me moderately well. My heathen code prescribes for me almost the identical rules of life which you have laid down for your ordinary Christian. As for resisting the Devil, and believing in Christ, your Bible makes it plain that no man does either the one or the other to any purpose, whose life does not proclaim his efforts to all the world. Unless, therefore, your model Christian be one who can be distinguished at a glance from his fellow-men, by his uncompromising abhorrence of evil, and his fearless devotion to his Master's name, — in which case he becomes at once *my* ideal of a true follower of Christ, and ceases to be yours, — we may leave out the two last items of your definition, and consider the others only. Well, then, like the Christian, I must work: if I don't, I am a sluggard, and not a man. Like him, I must be temperate in my habits: if not, I become a brute, and not an intellectual being. Like him, I must be civil and considerate: if not, I am a cur, and not a gentleman. All these things, however, I learn, not in any sense from Christianity, but from civilization. And it is of such men as myself that the decently behaved majority in your Christian world is composed. You have made an egregious mistake in calling this country of yours a Christian country. It is nothing of the sort. It is a genuine heathen country. Its principles are heathen; its policy is heathen; its laws are heathen. Look at that newspaper on the table. From the first column to the last it is utterly heathen; and it forms the expression of public opinion throughout the land. I am not abusing it. I delight in it. I read my 'Times' every day, and my 'Saturday' every week. I don't always agree with what they say, though I usually find, that, on most subjects of general interest, they take a sound and sensible view; but it is always a purely heathen view. The editors themselves would not pretend that it is otherwise. It is the view of writers who leave Christ entirely out of the question, who would never dream of stopping to consider what Christ might have to say about this or that. They would laugh at you, if you suggested such a thing. The public press is concerned with the rights of the people, the prosperity of the country, and the temporal welfare of mankind. It utterly ignores Christ and Christianity. And yet you Christians read it, regulate your opinion by it, and suffer it to influence insensibly your thoughts, your principles, your moral tone. And all the while you cannot doubt, that, if

Christ should come on earth again, the very first thing he would do would be to denounce the modern newspaper as godless and devilish and abominable. How could he do otherwise? Is it conceivable that Christ and 'The Times' should exist together? that He whose purpose it is to subdue the hearts of all men to himself should suffer them, at one and the same moment, to be subdued by a power so gigantic as the voice of public opinion? Could he permit, do you suppose, the discussion of creeds and doctrines on the heathen principle of common-sense, and not on the Christian principle of what God has chosen to reveal? Of course he could not: the two systems are as fire and water. And the very fact that you parsons allow 'The Times' to be brought to your house, shows plainly enough how you have abandoned Christianity, and drifted quietly into civilization. I do not blame you. I rejoice to think that you should have had the good sense to discard what I believe to be an obsolete and foolish superstition. But I am bound to say that the course you have taken seems to me one of very questionable honesty. Christ has told you to fight vigorously against the world: you have coolly made peace with it. Nay, he has declared this incessant conflict to be the very condition of your membership with him: you have repudiated the conditions, while yet you claim the membership. Christ has said that the joys of this life are wholly incompatible with the joys of the life to come: you Christians take your fill of pleasure on this earth, and expect to have pleasure also in heaven. In your amusements, you go just the length which we heathen go, and stop short exactly where we stop short, — at that point, namely, where pleasure begins to pall upon the fancy, and self-indulgence interferes with business or with health. Whatever delights common-sense permits to heathens, Christianity permits to Christians, and upon precisely the same terms, — that they be moderately indulged. Surely you cannot be honest in maintaining a position so extremely like our own. You ought to be fighting with us for your very life. I am very glad that you are not fighting. I greatly prefer peace to war. But, then, any child can see that you have made peace by the simple process of surrender. As Archdeacon Denison said the other day, we have heard a good deal lately about church defence: what we ought to be hearing about is church aggression. At present, the Church and the world get on as harmoniously together as if they had every interest and every principle in common. Look at your bench of bishops. There they are, some six and twenty of them, successors of Christ, specially appointed to take his place on earth till he comes to claim his kingdom. I should just like to know what single thing they are doing which he would do if he were here. There they are, pre-eminent among men, not for their humility, and the sanctity of their lives, but for their social rank, as peers of this mighty realm. There they are, with their five thousand pounds a year, and upwards, — an income not to be spent upon the spiritual wants of their respective dioceses, but upon themselves and their children. There they are, with their palaces in the country, and their mansions in Belgrave Square, dining pleasantly with their equals in the fashionable world, and never guilty, mark you, of such shocking bad taste as to denounce the frightful luxury of aristocratic life as a deadly sin, or tell a spendthrift nobleman to his face that such pursuits as pigeon-slaughtering and horse-racing are leading him anywhere else rather than to heaven. It is all very well for your archbishop to talk about converting us poor heathen. Let him try his hand, first, at the conversion of the house of lords. Why, if he would speak and act like his Master Christ, for one single week, he would not have a friend left in London. If he, and the rest of the bishops with him, would issue a solemn protest against the wickedness and extravagance of the rich, they would make themselves at once so absolutely offensive, that no man of wealth or rank would ever receive them into his house again. And this, and nothing less than this, as you know far better than I do, is what Christ would do."

"My dear Curtis," said I, trying to look horrified, "you should not talk in such a way about the dignitaries of the Church."

"Dignitaries of the Church, indeed! Why the very existence of such a class is a flat contradiction and insult to the teaching of Christ. If your 'dignitaries' want to convert the world, let them go about *in formâ pauperis*, and wash the saints' feet. But I perceive, my dear fellow, that you are determined to misunderstand my line. I tell you again that I, as a heathen, am perfectly satisfied with things as they are. I look upon your archbishop, and your bishops, and all your clergy, with profound respect. I think them an excellent, industrious, energetic, and gentlemanly set of men. All I say is, that they are not Christians: they are heathens. I do not say that they are savages. You good people have given heathenism such a bad name, that one is constantly obliged to stop short, and apologize for using it, and to explain that one does not contemplate the case of a gentleman in paint and feathers, who dines off his neighbor. When I speak of a heathen, as distinguished from a Christian, I intend no greater insult than when I say that a Prussian is not a Portuguese. I know very well what Christ was like; and I can see that your priests and bishops, as regards their attitude towards society, at least, are as unlike him as they can possibly be. They have absolutely nothing in common with him. They are outside his system altogether. They follow his teaching just so far as he taught principles which are common to Christians and heathen alike; and they cast him off at the very point where he becomes distinctively Christ, and ceases to be a mere philosopher. They are simply professors in a school, of which Christ was the historical founder, — a school, without question, the most perfect in organization, and the purest in morals, which the world has ever known; but a school, nevertheless, and nothing more. It will last its time, just as other schools have lasted; and then it will collapse, and give way to something better, or something, at any rate, which better suits the temper of the age. There are not wanting signs of such a dissolution even now. That which was to make Christian truth durable, nay, eternal, was just this, — that it was *not* a school of philosophy, but the kingdom of God; that it was not of earth, but of heaven; that it was not material or carnal, but spiritual, mysterious, supernatural. If Christianity be not literally this, it is nothing. If Christ be not absolute king of the hearts and consciences of men, he is nothing. If the graces and sacraments of Christ be not powerful enough to make his priests, amid countless infirmities of the flesh, the very and exact representation of himself to sinners, they are nothing. The moment you regard Christianity in the light of a secular philosophy, it breaks down; for the simple reason that it is contrary to common-sense, and does perpetual violence to the natural instincts of mankind. This feature of his teaching, as Christ himself took pains to show, is the one feature which separates that teaching from the philosophies, and makes it Christian. It cannot exist in the empire of the intellect and the region of human prosperity, because it came on purpose to destroy them both. It was expressly meant to be laughed at and scoffed at by unbelievers, just as Christ was laughed at and scoffed at in his day. Nobody laughs at Christianity in its popular modern phase: there is nothing left to laugh at. It has cast away all that was ridiculous in the sight of men, and has become decent and plausible and inoffensive. It does not dare so much as to hold its own against any nameless writer in 'The Times.' The obscurest heathen need only say that such and such a stern precept of Christ is contrary to the spirit of the age; and Christianity politely agrees with him, and drops that precept out of its moral code. My dear fellow, let us bring the matter to a test. Was not Christ laughed to scorn by one half of his unbelieving hearers, and cruelly persecuted by the other? "

"Yes, no doubt he was; but circumstances were then so very different. Men do not laugh at Christianity now, not because Christianity has changed, but because they have learned to believe in it. Christ has subdued them to himself; and the kingdoms of this world have become the kingdom of Christ."

"Will you dare to look me in the face and tell me so, when civilized society has made itself totally independent of Christ; when England, from north to south, has given herself over to luxury; and the sin of London alone cries out to Heaven a hundred-fold more loudly than the sin of Babylon, or Nineveh, or Tyre? Don't be angry with me, dear friend; but you parsons are so abominably unreal! The kingdoms of this world become the kingdom of Christ! Good gracious! Why, I never go to one of your churches, but the clergyman begins to preach about 'these dangerous days,' and protests with all his vigor that 'there never was a time when infidelity was so rampant, or vice so flagrant.' And now you have the assurance to tell me that Christ has subdued the world. It seems to me, that, when you want to make a point in your Sunday's sermon, you declare that we are all under the dominion of the Devil; and, when you are taunted with not having made much progress in the work of recovering us from his grasp, you admit that we are not so very bad, after all."

"Nevertheless," I answered, "there can be no doubt that Christianity was intended to accommodate itself to the laws of human progress and the changes of society. It could not be, now, in England, precisely the same as it was nearly two thousand years ago in Judæa. Besides, there are numerous sayings of our Lord, which were clearly never meant to be received in their literal sense."

"I deny that utterly," said Curtis in reply. "Your modern theory on this point is a bare-faced assumption, for which neither Christ, nor any one of the New-Testament writers, gives you the faintest spark of authority. Whatever he commanded, he expects you literally to perform; and you have no right to filter away his words until they enunciate a mere abstract piece of philosophic wisdom, which the heathen and the Christian may both alike accept. In the whole range of heathen history, I never yet heard of any thing so palpably dishonest as the way in which you Christians have repudiated the words of Christ. It passes my comprehension, how you can stand at your desk, and read a chapter out of the gospel, without sinking into the earth for shame. Every sentence of your lips condemns you. I won't insult you with quotations; but you must be able to recall verse upon verse of Christian precept, which you parsons have long ago agreed among yourselves to regard as obsolete and unpractical. To you, just as much as to us, Christianity and Christ have become ridiculous. My dear friend, if Christ were to come now in human flesh, how should you receive him?"

"I am scarcely bound," said I, "to answer a question so absurd. Christ could not come now. This is not the time appointed for his coming. He came when God saw fit to send him; and that time is past."

"Still, I suppose it is conceivable that God should have been pleased to send him now. What special unfitness of time or place should hinder his appearing next week in London, if it had been so decreed?"

"But it was not so decreed. Fitness of time and place made it necessary that he should appear in Bethlehem eighteen hundred and seventy years ago."

"Perhaps you think that the people in London are a little too civilized just now to make his appearance among them a success?"

"I think nothing about it. It could not possibly happen."

"Perhaps we good folks nowadays are a little too clever, just a trifle more knowing, don't you see, than might have been convenient."

"Don't talk in such a horrible way!" said I; for I felt that the man was becoming blasphemous.

"Then I am to understand," continued he, "that Christ could only have come to earth successfully, on condition of his choosing an obscure country, and hitting upon a time when there were no special correspondents to find out all about him, no photographers to show us exactly what he was like, and no telegraphic wires to carry his words of wisdom from one continent to another? If you, a minister of Christ, are prepared to admit as much as this, you can hardly wonder that intelligent laymen should disbelieve."

"Since you press me," said I, "perhaps one reason in the divine counsels might have been this,—that the Son of God should be spared the additional insults and indignities to which his appearance in a civilized country would have exposed him."

"Ah! now we are coming to the point. And what would those additional insults and indignities be? What should you Christians do to Christ if he came to London?"

"Believe in him, of course. Why, do you really suppose that we should crucify him?"

"No, you would not crucify him: it is not the custom of the day. But I tell you what you would do. You would laugh at him, and hoot at him, and have him locked up in a madhouse. He would offend you, every bit as much as he offended the scribes and Pharisees. He would interfere with your life every bit as much as he interfered with theirs. His persistent, uncompromising abhorrence of the mildest form of sin would appear just as extravagant to you as it did to Herod. It seems to me, my friend, that the blind, benighted heathen has given you a tolerably fair test by which to try your Christianity. You have no right whatever to say that Christ could not have come in 1872;

and the fact that you think the idea so foolish casts a very grave suspicion on the sincerity of your own belief. It is a relief to you to recollect that an event so extraordinary took place at a time when the observation of men was not quite so acute as it is now, and when the credentials of the chief actor in the scene were not likely to be too critically or scientifically examined. You have not courage to face the contemplation of a poor despised figure walking wearily through the streets of some modern city, and claiming to be your Lord. You feel by no means certain that you would not laugh at him as he passed along. And so you pretend, that, although such a visitation would be unfitting now, it was fitting enough eighteen hundred years ago. What wonder, as I said before, that when you, who profess to believe the gospel, are glad to thrust as far away from you as possible the vision of a personal, living Christ, men of a doubting or speculative turn of mind should find it hard to persuade themselves that he ever lived at all? But, in shirking thus the difficulties of your belief, you do not ultimately escape them. If God had so designed it, Christ might, with perfect fitness, have come to London in this present year. There is nothing whatever in the condition of our modern society which forbids such an hypothesis to stand. Civilization would, indeed, have made some difference in the form of insult cast upon him, and in the mode of death which he should eventually die; but civilization could make no difference in this, — that, whenever and wherever he appeared, he would have done violence to the tastes and habits of the vast majority of mankind. A tiny band would have clung to him in England, just as a tiny band clung to him in Galilee; but, to society at large, he must ever have been a positive offence, and to your pleasant gentlemanly priests and bishops the most palpable offence of all."

"I don't think you have any right to say so," objected I; "but it is useless to argue such a question. Of course, if he had come in this present century, he would have come in a totally different form."

"In what form? In the form of a modern prelate, softly clad, and sleek, with a couple of palaces, and fifteen thousand pounds a year? I very particularly doubt it. Whatever guise he took, it would be that of one whom men despise; whatever words he spoke, they would be words which make men gnash their teeth to hear; whatever deeds he wrought, they would be deeds so flatly opposed to worldly sense and worldly wisdom, as to cover him with ridicule and abuse. In such a guise, and with such words and deeds, unless the whole story of his life is an imposture, he must infallibly be dwelling among his people still. You have read your gospel superficially indeed, if you have not gathered from it this, — that whereas the philosophers could but teach, and establish a sect, and die, Christ would abide with his Church forever. Patriarchs and prophets had striven darkly and dimly to represent God to man; and they had failed. Christ was now to produce a form of testimony altogether new, — a testimony real, ever present, personal, — a testimony which should proclaim the truth as plainly in modern Paris, or London, or Berlin, as in Jerusalem or Galilee of old. Henceforth, men were not to hear of God, but to see him, — to see him, triumphing in every martyr's death, glorified by each confessor's courage, shining in the pure devotion of his faithful priests, winsome with the grace and loveliness of holy women who had dedicated their lives to him. Herein, and herein alone, does Christ become any thing better than the founder of a school. He is risen, you say; he has ascended up again to heaven. But his Spirit, if he be Christ at all, must linger here; and, if his Spirit has any strength that can rightly be called divine, it must be manifesting him with a brightness which cannot be hid, wherever his saints and children dwell. Tell me, my friend, whereabouts such a place may be. It is not in your churches, where congregations of good-natured, worldly-minded men and women offer up prayers to God, with lips so insincere, that they might just as well be offering them up to Jupiter. It is not in your bishops' palaces, where the apostles of a homeless, footsore Jesus maintain with befitting pomp and circumstance the dignity of the episcopal chair. It is not in the snug country parsonage, where the rector has settled himself comfortably in the midst of rural poverty and distress, and his charming wife and daughters fare sumptuously every day. Such men, believe me, cannot be Christ to the thirsty, perishing multitudes; and, because they are not Christ, they are nothing. That which men were yearning for, as the fulness of God's time drew near, was personal witness. Christ came, and gave it them. That which men are yearning for now, crying for from street and garret and death-bed, aye, and from the closet of the student searching after truth, and the haunts of the man of fashion, who would fain be something better than he is, is personal witness. You Christian priests won't give it them. You persistently withhold it. You dare not be to the world what Christ was. You boast that your religion suffers you to live as other men, to enjoy the pleasures of society, and indulge in moderation your natural desires, just as the well-conducted layman may. You have not the pluck to tell the squire to his face that his life from Sunday to Sunday, purposeless, idle, frivolous, if nothing worse, is a disgrace to your Christian village, and a transgression of the law of God. You dare not tell him so: if you did, he might, with some propriety, retort that your life was but little different from his own.

"I can't see why you should say that the average squire's life is a bad life."

"I don't say it is a bad life: I say it is not a Christian life. It is the life of a good-natured, gentlemanly heathen. Look at the ordinary pursuits of such a man. One of the best of them probably will be fox-hunting"—

"And a thoroughly noble, manly pastime too."

"Extremely noble, for fifty red-coated heroes to chase a wretched little quadruped from cover to cover, and from field to field, watching the hungry dogs as they drive the breath inch by inch out of his body, till at last they fall upon their victim, and (as your great authority, the *Reverend* Mr. Daniel, says they ought to do if they are decently trained hounds) *devour him ferociously!* As a matter of opinion, I confess that I call such sport brutal and cowardly. Nevertheless, if it be found necessary, in order to keep the country gentleman at home, and attach him to his tenantry, I can afford to admit, from a heathen point of view, that the end justifies the means. But how such a sport can be designated as Christian is more than I can understand. Is it possible to imagine Christ, under any conceivable circumstances, taking pleasure in hunting an animal to death? In a Christian aspect, such a pursuit has not even the excuse of supplying a needful occupation, because the squire ought to be fully occupied already in improving the cottages of his poor, building alms-houses for the aged, beautifying, to the full extent of his resources, the temple wherein he worships his God, and preparing his soul for the judgment-day. These are the Christian duties of a country gentleman. But you parsons dare not tell him so. He would call you a parcel of old women; and you prefer to stand well with him, and to be thought muscular and manly. I was told, not long ago, by one whose person and office I cannot but respect, — I was told, as a thing much to be admired, of a certain exemplary squire who was accustomed to ride home from hunting, towards the hour of evensong, by way of the parish church, throw his bridle to the groom, enter the sacred building, put on a surplice over his scarlet coat, and read the lessons for the minister. All I can say is, that this gentleman's ideas of right and wrong, if, indeed, he had any ideas at all, must have been jumbled together in such inextricable confusion, that I wonder the very effort of thinking did not drive him mad. And, concerning the parson who encouraged a phase of Christianity so peculiar, I will only remark, that the fact of such a scene being permitted to take place, with the sanction, apparently, of the bishop, and the general approval of churchmen, justifies in every point my opinion, that your modern average priests are veritable heathen philosophers, and not ministers of Christ at all."

"Then you think that priests are bound to be mild and spooney?"

"I think they are bound to be like Christ. I don't know whether you would call him mild and spooney: I more than half suspect that you would. And I think, moreover, that it is in the highest degree dishonest to claim the possession of gifts which are essentially spiritual, mysterious, and of a totally different world, and all the while to maintain a muscularity of thought and action which is purely and entirely heathen. Cherish your muscularity, by all means, — the more you preach and practise it, I say, the better, — but do have the simple candor to confess that you have stolen it direct from heathenism, and that the whole current of Christ's example sets absolutely the other way."

"According to your ideas, then, a parson ought never to go into society at all. Now, I totally disagree with you. It would be a most disastrous thing for our people that we should refuse to meet them in friendly intercourse. The presence of the clergy raises at once the tone of secular conversation. And Christ's example bears me out in this; for he not only attended a marriage-feast, but incurred the nick-name of a wine-bibber, who ate and drank with publicans and sinners."

"Yes," returned my friend: "those are instances, no doubt, very few and far between, in which Christ may be said to have sanctioned some approach towards convivial life; and I am bound to say that you modern Christians have made the most of them. One hears them quoted everywhere. But what took Christ to Cana of Galilee? Why, he went there to perform one of the very greatest of his mighty works, the immense significance of which, in connection with later events, I need scarcely point out to a clergyman. And, as for his dining with publicans and sinners, do you suppose he went among them to enjoy himself, or to preach the gospel? And for which of these reasons, may I ask, do you parsons mix so freely with the world? What single feature is there in common between his alleged conviviality and yours? Is it from his example that you borrow your half-hours of affable conversation about nothing whatever; your friendly intercourse, wherein the chances of doing good are as one to twenty, and the chances of talking a vicious amount of non-sense are as twenty to one; your dinner-parties, in the midst of which the priest is pleasantly supposed to stand up suddenly, to the consternation of his host, and rebuke ex-travagance and self-indulgence and frivolous words, but never yet was known to do any thing of the kind; your archery-meetings, croquet-tournaments, five-o'clock teas, and other modes of innocent recreation, which you pat-ronize with the laudable intent of showing how possible it is to serve God and mammon, how easy to combine the pleasures of this world with those of the world to come? And then you talk of raising the tone of conversation! Why, my good friend, you know perfectly well that the parson goes into society on the very same footing as that on which the layman goes, because he is a gentleman, and it is pleasant to meet him. If he dared to reprove and exhort, or assume any priestly function, his friends would declare that he was not a gentleman, and would invite him no more. His clerical duties, so far as they may be exercised at all, are strictly limited to the saying of grace before and after dinner. And the fashion in which this ceremony is performed shows plainly enough the amount of respect in which his office is held. He mutters some mysterious words, of which nobody takes the slightest possible notice; and there his business ends. If he presumed to keep the company waiting while he offered up a decently earnest prayer, he would stand but little chance of being asked to say grace again. Try the experiment yourself, old fellow, when next you go out to dine. Speak up from the fulness of your heart, as you contemplate the bountiful feast spread out before you, and thank Him in fitting language to whom you believe that thanks are due. No, no. You dare not utter a syllable which would hurt the prejudices of your friends. And all the while you call yourself the minister of Christ; of Christ, who was perpetually doing the very thing which you will not do, — rebuking, irritating, offending, nay, positively insulting, men with his precepts, if, by any means, — by gentleness or by severity, by love or by fear, by entreaty or by threatening, — he might drag them away from their deadly, damning sins, and win them to himself, and make them good and pure."

"And yet," said I, "if you would go somewhere and hear a course of Lenten sermons, I don't think you would have much cause to complain of our not speaking out with sufficient boldness and severity."

"Sermons," repeated Curtis, — "oh, ah! I have no fault to find with *them.* Your preaching is plain enough, and your Sunday standard of Christian holiness all that can be desired. You can afford to *preach* Christ, partly because, with the Bible in your hands, you could scarcely do less; and partly because, such is your confirmed unreality, it has come to be generally understood that the precepts of pulpit oratory are to be very cautiously applied. You preach Christ, and then you have done with him. When you meet your flock on week-days, you meet them as other men. You are just as proud as other men, if you happen to be second cousin to an honorable, or on terms of intimacy with a lord. You are just as fond of your dinner as other men, and make quite as much fuss if the mutton is under-done. You are every whit as irritable as other men, and take offence as readily, if any one insults you. I have known dignitaries of the Church cut a man dead for six months, because he had offered them some trumpery affront. Christ, I am inclined to fancy, would have met one who had done him an injury, with a kindlier greeting than before."

"My good friend," interrupted I, fast losing my temper at the man's absurd Utopianism, "you cannot expect impossibilities. We parsons don't set up for angels. We are men of like passions with yourselves. All that we can pretend to do is to behave like Christian gentlemen, and set a good example to the world."

"What example?"

"The example of Christ."

"Just so. And Christ does not begin to become Christ in your hands at all, until you have lifted him far above the region of gentlemanly behavior, and brought him to the point where he is a positive nuisance to the natural man. You cannot be setting the example of Christ, while men speak well of you, and seek your company, and find your tone and habits very much like their own. The squire, the soldier, the good-natured, agreeable fellow whose wine you drink and at whose jokes you laugh, — these men, unless you have already done your work upon them, and humbled them at the feet of Christ, ought to feel your presence an intolerable restraint, and toss their heads impatiently at the very sound of your name. You ought to be besieging them, worrying them, literally *boring* them, with the vehemence of your entreaties that they will come out from the plague and pestilence, and save their souls from hell. But no. It is more gentlemanly to let them linger in their sin, and die. And haven't you the wit to perceive, my dear old friend, that, to whatever extent you abstain from open war against the vice and slothfulness of every man you meet, to precisely the same extent you are a mere excrescence on society? Unless you are making worldly men and women hate you just as they hated Christ, you are simply a superfluous body of men. Civilization does not want you. The laws by which she keeps brutality in check, and brings the drunkard and the murderer to justice, were framed without you. She has police to clear her streets, and magistrates to convict the vagabond and the rogue, and a keen sense of the honorable and the upright to regulate her intercourse between man and man" —

"Which she borrowed from Christianity."

"Which she borrowed from nothing of the kind; which belongs to her, on the contrary, as a matter of decent human feeling, and without which a man becomes a savage and a beast."

"It did not belong to the Greeks and Romans before Christ came."

"I defy you to prove it. All our relics of classical antiquity tell a different tale. We have but left the Athenian behind in manufactures and money-making, just as he had left the Israelite behind in literature and the arts of war.

From the Queen of Sheba to Queen Victoria, from Solomon to Mr. Robert Lowe, the course of this world has developed a steady progress in civilization, with which progress Christianity — I mean not Christian philosophy, but the Christianity of Christ — has had nothing whatever to do. Will you presume to tell me that our last-acquired colony is civilized because the missionary landed there and spoke of Christ, and not because merchants sent a cargo there, and opened to the inhabitants the resources of a flourishing trade?"

"Look here, old fellow," interrupted I, "I won't sit still and hear you abusing missionaries."

"I am not abusing missionaries. You persist in misinterpreting me. Heathen as I am, I could kiss the feet of any man who leaves home and friends, and the softnesses of life, and takes the cross in his hand, and becomes Christ to the poor and needy, whether in Polynesia, or Shoreditch, or Bermondsey. But I won't admit that missionary work has civilized the world. My dear fellow, where have your clergy worked the harder, — in Whitechapel, or in Grosvenor Square?"

"In Whitechapel, I should suppose."

"And which place is the more civilized of the two? Why, if Christianity has any thing to do with Christ at all, civilization must ever be its deadliest foe. The two forces labor in totally different fields. Christianity wins souls for heaven: civilization wins prosperity for men on earth. Christianity works for the glory of God: civilization does not pretend to take any such object into account, but simply works for the glorification of human talent, and the success of human enterprise. Instead of marching hand in hand, as the cant of the day would represent, they ought to be fighting tooth and nail; and the fact that they have ceased to fight proves that one or the other of them has given in. I had the curiosity, not long ago, to attend one of your monster festivals of the Society for the Propagation of the Gospel, at which some learned bishop was the appointed preacher. 'Think, my brethren,' said the excellent man, — 'think how the words of our Master have been fulfilled! See how, in every corner of the globe, on the boundless continent, and among the islands of the mighty ocean, the Christian Church has made its way! To all the nations of the earth the glad tidings have gone forth; and Europe, Asia, Africa, and America have owned the dominion of Christ.' I thought I had never heard such a piece of cool impertinence in all my life. Why, it is the English merchantman, and not the missionary, that has subdued the nations of the earth. The missionary — all honor to him! — has made a handful of converts at Graham's Town or Madagascar, just as he has made a handful at Haggerstone or the London Docks; but the reason why vast continents and colonies profess the British faith is because they are under the government of the British crown. Your modern Christianity has denied Christ, repudiated as obsolete more than half his distinctive teaching, declared his example to be antiquated and unsuited to modern times, grown ashamed of his social rank, and calmly assumed, without one scrap of authority, that his weary, drooping, threadbare figure is fitly represented by the well-fed rector, the pompous, self-important dignitary, and the croquet-playing, dog-cart-driving curate, of a polished generation, —your Church, I say, has done all this; and then it has the unblushing impudence to claim the spread of civilization, and the triumphs of man's industry and genius, as the fruits of its own labor in Christ's name!"

"Of course they are the fruits of its own labor. Christianity has left its mark over all the world. Every art, every science, every social pursuit of man, has become impregnated with it; and it is simply foolish to take your stand outside the system, as if you were indebted to it for nothing. You cannot so much as date a letter, without tacitly admitting your belief in the birth of Christ."

"Quite so. And I may just as well say that you cannot look up at the stars, without tacitly admitting your belief in Mars and Venus; or that you cannot name the days of the week, without tacitly acknowledging a host of Saxon deities. No doubt, Christianity has left its mark over all the world; and so has heathenism. There never was a philosophy yet, which did not leave its mark; and the teaching of Christ, the best of all philosophies, has left more permanent marks than any. No educated heathen would hesitate to confess how much society owes to the civilizing effects of Christianity. But you will not have it so. You say that Christ was not a civilizer. You say that he was God; and that, so far from coming to make this world pleasant and polite, he came to demonstrate the utter worthlessness of all things therein; that, so far from ministering to human progress, he taught that the more men learn, and the more they labor, and the more they get, the farther do they go astray from him, and the weaker does their hope become of everlasting life hereafter. This is your doctrine; and I say that, having chosen it, you ought to abide by it. My complaint against you is, that you only use it when it happens to be convenient, and at all other times are content to put up with heathenism. When you are preaching a sermon, or saying your prayers, or talking about missionary work, or 'shutting up' a sceptic, you take the loftiest possible ground, and discourse of miracles, and spiritual agencies, and the marvellous death and resurrection of Christ, and the eternal joys of heaven, or flames of hell; but when we turn your own words upon you, and suggest that such extraordinary beliefs involve extraordinary lives, you back out of your Christianity at once, as regards its supernatural features, and stand upon it only as upon a very good philosophy; which is what we admitted it to be all along. We heathen are content to be honest and truthful and kind and courteous and moral. You Christians come to us, and say that this is not enough, but that, in addition to all this, we must follow Christ. We strongly object to follow him, because we are not prepared to renounce this agreeable world, and to be hated and laughed at for our eccentricities, as he was: so we decline. Whereupon, you call us unbelievers and atheists, and all sorts of names; while you yourselves object to follow Christ precisely as much as we do, and from precisely the same cause. I call this dishonest and illogical. Having made choice of an unearthly Guide, you should be content to follow him along unearthly paths; and if, in following him, you find yourselves committed to a life which ordinary people regard as the life of a lunatic, you should put up with the inconvenience of being considered lunatics so long as you continue in this lower world, and look forward to getting credit for being in your right senses when you reach a better world above. But this does not suit you. You claim the privilege of doing exactly as we do all the week, and keep your mystical beliefs to hurl at our heads on Sunday."

"My dear fellow," answered I, "your argument comes round and round to the same thing again and again, and simply amounts to this, — that the Christian, like any other man, is of necessity inconsistent."

"Pardon me," replied he: "inconsistency has nothing to do with the matter. Inconsistency implies that a man makes some sort of effort to do what he thinks right, and fails, and tries again. My point is, that you make, and profess to make, no effort of any kind. I should call it an inconsistency, if, having admitted that the imitation of Christ forbade your enjoyment of earthly pleasures, you were seen, once in a way, at Newmarket or Evans's. But I cannot call it an inconsistency that there should be nothing whatever in your present religious code to prevent, let us say, the Christian, the man who denies that Christ ever lived, and the man who never by any chance offers up a prayer, from being associated together on equal terms in business, in pleasure, in every conceivable relation of life, in such a way as to make it simply impossible, unless you watch their pursuits on Sunday, to tell which is which. I cannot call it an inconsistency that all Christian England should wink at idolatry, the distinctive sin of ancient heathenism, and the greatest of all abominations in the sight of God, and should systematically teach young boys a mass of lies and folly about gods and goddesses who never lived, because the Alcestis or the Iliad is better Greek than Chrysostom on St. Matthew. I cannot call it an inconsistency that Christian sculptors should not care two straws, so long as they can get an order, whether they set to work upon an infant Bacchus or an infant Christ. I call these things deliberate abandonments of principle; and they are beautifully characteristic of your entire modern Christianity. If you really believed a whole roomful of worldly-minded people to be threatened with unquenchable fire, it would be impossible for you to help betraying your belief; for you could never open your mouth to speak to them on any other subject than the frightful peril in which they lay. And, if you really believed in Christ as any thing better than a wise instructor, you would burn every mythological book, and break in pieces every mythological statue, and call your glorious stars, which speak to you so eloquently of the great Creator's power, by some better names than the names of fabulous absurdities, whose very remembrance is an insult to the majesty of God."

"Really, Curtis," said I, "you talk like some old woman."

"Nay," answered he, "these sentiments are none of mine. *I* don't talk like an old woman. But *you* ought to talk like one; and because you are ashamed to be heard talking like one, and dread, above all things, that the world should taunt you with old womanish ideas, you have dropped out of your theology whatever grates against common-sense, and appear inoffensively before society as a civilized heathen. What I cannot get you to understand is, that in so doing, in this futile attempt of yours to represent as manly and muscular a system which is essentially meek and mild, you have abandoned the distinctive principle of your faith, and given up the whole point between the world and Christ, and have turned a kingdom of mysteries into a school of morals; in which school, you clergy, having abjured the peculiarities of your weary, sorrow-stricken Master, have become the mere professors of a good and sound philosophy, — the philosophy of common-sense in business, and gentlemanly conduct in society; but I don't know that we particularly need your services, because any intelligent, honorable layman can teach such a philosophy equally well. A national church is a very expensive article; and unless you have something better to tell us than we can learn any day at luncheon, from the lawyer or the squire, it is high time that you should retire from clerical life, and earn your bread elsewhere. Men are pleased to call you *Reverend;* but, if such a title belongs to any profession on this earth, it belongs not to the parson, but to the doctor. He it is, who, in some degree at least, is making himself Christ to the suffering and the sorrowing among mankind. He it is who turns out of his bed at midnight to cool the poor man's burning lips, or succor a woman with the tenderest efforts of his skill, who can never pay him sixpence for his trouble, whether her infant lives or dies."

"I am sure I hope that I should go and visit any one who sent for me, just as readily as the doctor does."

"I have not a doubt of it; only, what you would do cheerfully enough once in a way, he does as a matter of business all day long. Your work is baby's play compared with his; and I really don't know what class of society would be very much the worse, if the entire fifteen or twenty thousand of you were swept off the face of the earth to-morrow. We don't want you, my friend, indeed, we don't, if you are only going to help us, in some infinitesimal degree, to become more civilized and polite and human. Be Christ to us, and at any rate we shall understand you. We may laugh at you, and call you enthusiasts, and decline to become sharers of your unattractive life; but we shall reject your teaching at our own risk: the consequences, if consequences there be, will fall upon ourselves; and, at the very least, we shall understand you. We cannot understand you now. We have not the faintest notion what it is that you want us to do. Your sermons tell us of one sort of Christ, and your conversation of another. In your gospel we see a Christ bruised, and covered with reproach, and laughed to scorn: in your daily life we see a Christ who has grown ashamed of his poverty and low estate, has cast off the garb of the Man of sorrows, and has become a courteous gentleman, or a shrewd business-like man of the world. And, because we see these things, we don't believe in any Christ at all. You are fond of preaching about the spirit of modern infidelity, and love to flatter yourselves that some half a dozen rationalistic Germans are responsible for all the scepticism of the day. Let me tell you that the un-Christ-like priest is the truest source of infidelity. The free discussion of theological difficulties could shake no one's faith, if the witness of the clergy to the truth of their own gospel were such as any reasonable man could entertain. Why should I believe, when, as far as my powers of penetration are able to assist me, I can see that you yourselves are only half persuaded to be Christians?"

"I am afraid, my dear fellow," answered I, "that such an excuse will not help you. God will call you to account for your unbelief, whether we preach faithfully or no. You have your Bible" —

"The Bible is of no use without an interpreter. If a Bible could be picked up somewhere among the 'islands of the mighty ocean,' do you suppose that the poor benighted heathen would understand a word of it? The Bible lays down injunctions which no Christian man or woman of my acquaintance pretends to fulfil; and, when I ask for an explanation of such a peculiar fact, you mystify me to that extent that I don't know where I am. You tell me that one-half, at least, of the express commands of Christ were not intended to be literally obeyed; and that when he said to one who would devote himself to his service, 'Sell that thou hast, and give to the poor, and take up thy cross and follow me,' he *meant* to say, 'Buy through some clerical agent the advowson of a fat rectory within an easy distance of town, look out for some nice young lady with a little money of her own, and make yourself thoroughly comfortable.'"

"Stay," said I, "you have hit upon an acknowledged abuse. Most of us condemn traffic in church-patronage as a scandal."

"Then, why don't your bishops dare to set to work and stop it? Why don't they boldly refuse to institute any man who has bought himself a living, and take the consequences? It would not do, would it? Why, they would gain at once the character of cantankerous, unsafe men, and lose their chance of that golden prize of vapid, stagnant moderation, — the see of C——."

"I had hoped, my dear Curtis, that you were too generous-hearted to impute unworthy motives, even to an adversary."

"Then, I beg to retract my words; and I take refuge in the only alternative left to me. Since your stern, single-minded prelates witness perpetually the transactions of which I speak, and do not interfere with them, I will assume that they see little in them to disapprove; that they have tacitly accepted the modern Christian theory, that the priesthood is a mere secular profession, in which a capitalist may invest his money, and look for profitable returns; and that the priest is a doctor of morals, just as other men are doctors of physic or of law."

"Perhaps," answered I, "our bishops think the practice a necessary evil; and, really, I do not see how it can be avoided. It makes very little difference, as far as I can judge, whether a man gets his father to buy him a living, or asks his friend to give him one."

"Very little difference indeed. The whole system under which rectories and canonries are treated as comfortable sources of income is purely and exclusively heathen."

"And yet our Lord himself allows that the laborer is worthy of his hire."

"Of how much hire? Why, of that amount exactly which is needful for his support while laboring, and of nothing further. Here is another of the texts which you perpetually have the impudence to misquote, as an apology for clerical self-indulgence. It so happens that the words tell expressly against you. Christ was bidding his ministers go forth without purse or scrip or shoes, in a state of such utter poverty, that they were forced to live on the hospitality of their converts; and this, the bare food and lodging offered them, is what he permits them to accept as their legitimate reward. My dear friend, so long as you parsons twist about the words of Scripture after such a fashion as this, you can hardly wonder that a heathen like myself should decline to receive the Bible as a trustworthy witness of God."

"But there are other witnesses. Does not your own conscience tell you, every time you do any thing wrong, that there is a God who will sooner or later punish you?"

"Certainly not. *Your* conscience tells you so, probably enough, because you have drunk in the belief with every breath of childhood, and learned it by heart upon your mother's lap. You are making some slight confusion, my friend, between conscience and deeply-rooted prejudice. I thoroughly believe in Nemesis, if that is what you mean. If I take too much sherry at night, I shall have a headache in the morning; and if I play a mean trick upon my neighbor, or cheat at cards, I shall have the satisfaction of remembering, for the rest of my life, that I have acted like a blackguard. All heathen believe in Nemesis, and some of them have canonized her as a deity; but such a belief has not much in common with your idea of God."

"Who do you suppose made the world?" I inquired, flattering myself that I had puzzled him at last.

"I am sure I don't know," answered he. "I should imagine that it came into existence by some mysterious law of generation, just as I came into existence myself. I am not bound to believe that the hands of any personal creator fashioned it, any more than I believe that the hands of any personal creator fashioned me."

"Then you really think it more reasonable to suppose that the sun and moon and stars got into their appointed places by chance, than that they were created, and are continually kept in check, by some almighty power?"

"I don't say that they came by chance. I presume that they were developed out of matter; and matter, like the principle of generation, is, of course, eternal."

"How can matter be eternal? Somebody must have made it."

"And how can somebody be eternal? Somebody else must have made *him*. My dear fellow, there are heaps of marvellous things in nature, which must needs be accepted, whether we will or no; but this much is certain, that, if you come to talk of reason, the most unreasonable belief of all is, that the world we see around us is the work of a personal and living God. Nay, it is precisely twice as difficult to believe that God made Nature, as to believe that Nature made herself: because, if Nature be final and supreme, you have one great mystery to perplex you; but if God made Nature out of nothing, when you have duly contemplated an effort so extraordinary, you must face the further problem, whence came God. The orthodox argument on this point is peculiar. You are forbidden to suppose, as a thing supremely ridiculous, that Nature herself is eternal, because so wonderful a piece of mechanism as the universe bears the manifest impress of an almighty hand. And yet you are not only permitted to hold, but are enjoined to believe steadfastly, on peril of damnation forevermore, that the almighty hand itself bears no impress whatever; that a Being many thousand times more wonderful than earth and sun and stars, inasmuch as he created them by the breath of his mouth, never had any beginning at all. Why it should be irrational to believe in the eternity of a substance, and not irrational to believe in the eternity of a person, one does not precisely understand. Give me some decently plausible evidence, and I will do my best to become convinced; but you can hardly expect me to believe in a God whom nobody has ever seen, who lives nobody can tell where, and is doing nobody knows what, simply because you show me the sun in heaven, and ask me how it got there. God himself has never asked any man to believe on evidence so absurd. Admitting your Bible to be true, I find him indeed appealing to the works of his creation as tokens of his power, but only doing so when he would confirm the wavering faith of those who already, in some degree, acknowledged him. It is one thing for a Christian or a Jew to worship with increased fervor when he contemplates the works of God: it is quite another thing for a heathen to evolve for himself the conception of a creator, because he does not know how else creation came. That witness of himself which God offered to the nations, when he sent them fruitful seasons, filling their hearts with food and gladness, — this,. as St. Paul confesses, was so palpably insufficient, that it became necessary to adopt some other way. So far, indeed, from expecting man to find him out by observing the ordinary course of Nature, the Almighty took special care, whenever he desired to make himself known, to upset the ordinary course of Nature, and work a miracle. From the burning bush and the plagues of Egypt, down to the draught of fishes a hundred and fifty and three, your Bible is a continuous record of events wherein God proved himself to be divine, by superseding the operations of the visible world. Such testimony could not fail to convince all but the wilfully obstinate and rebellious; and I, not being obstinate or rebellious, shall be only too happy to own myself convinced, if I may be shown such testimony now."

"Such testimony cannot be shown now. The age of miracles is passed."

"Excuse me," replied Curtis, "if I say that that sounds very suspiciously like a shuffle. If miracles are the accepted evidence of God's power, they must needs be repeated whenever

God's power is called in question. And it is called in question at the present day. 'There never was a time,' according to your favorite burst of pulpit eloquence, 'when infidelity made such rapid strides.' Well, then, show us wicked infidels a miracle. Let us see Nebuchadnezzar turned into an ox, or hear a dumb animal talking to its rider, or" —

"My dear fellow, I tell you that the Almighty does not see fit to work miracles now."

"And why? Because people are a little too sharp to be taken in by them? Because the special correspondent or the policeman would be one too many on the scene? My good friend, it is of the very essence of a miracle, as evidence, that men should *see* it. It is of no use second-hand. A miracle that you hear of, but did not see, becomes at once a myth. Your scripture stories about Joshua's sun and moon, or the passage of the Israelites through the water, are in themselves not one atom less ridiculous to posterity than the classical fables about Zeus and Aphrodite. Let those who saw them believe in them. You clever Christian folk must take us heathen for a pack of fools. You tell us of some outrageously incredible events, which took place at a highly convenient distance off, in the very backwoods of history, and under circumstances which it is simply impossible to investigate; and when we modestly shake our heads, and ask for a repetition of the marvel, you coolly dismiss us with the answer, that, in this enlightened age, a miracle could not be performed."

"A miracle could be performed easily enough, if God willed it. But such a method of proof has become unnecessary: God has revealed himself in these last days by his Son."

"Precisely so. Now we shall understand each other. He has revealed himself by his Son. Nature, as a primary instructor, tells me nothing about God whatever. Forced, in any case, to accept the world around me as a mystery, I find the supposition that creation made itself to be the least unfathomable mystery of all. The Bible, as a primary instructor, tells me nothing about God whatever. For all I know, its chronicles may be Hebrew myths, its prophecies written to order, *ex post facto*, by some clever Jew, and its New Testament the code of morals of an elaborate and impudent superstition. Let those for whom such evidence was produced accept it, if they please; for myself, it is Christ, and only Christ, who can tell me any thing about God which I care to know. If the age of miracles has ceased, it must be because the age of personal witness has begun. Never yet was man asked to believe in a supernatural God, without evidence supernatural. This is the evidence which I demand, and which, look where I will, I cannot get. Show me Christ, and he shall be my testimony about God. Why cannot you produce him? If ever he came on earth, he *must* be here. If he has gone away from you, and left his people all alone, the age of miracles must needs begin again, or men will rightly disbelieve. The modern Christian talks of belief in God, as if it were the easiest thing on earth. Why, it is the very highest effort of the human mind. It involves a struggle between faith and reason, whose intensity can only be measured by the magnitude of the truths embraced. The unseen and the infinite baffle me, bewilder me, distract me: only by some infallible proof can I be persuaded of their reality. Such proof I should discover in the working of a miracle before my eyes. You tell me that I cannot have such proof. Then I will have personal witness. I will have that testimony by which miracles in the physical world were superseded, when, in the spiritual world (if there be a spiritual world) God proclaimed a kingdom whose life and progress should be the mightiest miracle of all, — the kingdom of Christ in the hearts of men. I won't be put off with a reference to some historical book, which may or may not be true. I won't be put off by being asked to explain how the trees yield their fruit, or the earth goes round. The Bible may do much to confirm my faith when I have once confessed it; and the study of Nature may kindle my gratitude and raise my heart towards Him whom I have once brought myself to worship as the maker of all the worlds. But, in a matter of such overwhelming import, I choose, in the first instance, to have testimony which cannot be denied. If

I am to believe in God, it must be because I see him in Christ: if I am to believe in Christ, it must be because I see him in Ignatius, in Augustine, in Bernard of Clairvaux; because there are men and women living on this earth, on whom he has left his mark so visibly, that it cannot be mistaken, — men and women as firmly persuaded of his death upon the cross, as if their own eyes had seen him die. And what do you think must be the life and conversation of one who has seen him die; who knows, moreover, as your sermons teach us, that his own sins, his own wilful indulgence of appetite or desire, were the sins which put his Saviour to death; who is conscious, at every moment of the day, that he himself is verily guilty of the murder of his God? Don't be shocked, dear fellow, if my language is plain and strong. I am but showing you the legitimate issue of your own doctrine. You gentlemen like to have the theology all to yourselves, so that you may stop short whenever you approach dangerous ground, and refrain from pushing an awkward truth to its natural conclusion. Permit a simple-minded layman to drive the argument home, and force you for once to abide by the results of your pulpit-teaching. I say, then, that every Christian man or woman who has ever sinned has with his own hand slain his God. If the death of Christ does not literally amount to this, it is a sentiment, a stage-rehearsal, a sham. You killed him, I killed him, every light-hearted, jovial English gentleman killed him; or else his crucifixion is a myth. Now, I ask you to tell me honestly whether your life, or the life of one Christian in ten thousand, is the life of a man whose mind is burdened with such a crime. Did you, or did you not, crucify Christ?"

"My dear Curtis, you put things in such a shocking way, that I hardly know what answer to give you."

"All the same I will trouble you to give me one."

"Well, I suppose, if it comes to that, I *did* crucify him."

"And yet you can sit there, and smoke your pipe, and drink your soda and brandy; and go to bed, and sleep as calmly as a child; and wake in the morning, and enjoy your life as merrily as if you had never hurt a fly."

"To be sure I can. What is the use of moping? I can't help having crucified Christ; and I sha'n't undo any harm that I have done, by making myself miserable and glum."

"It is not a question of undoing harm: it is a question of manifesting a commonly decent sorrow for the commission of a most atrocious deed."

"But, my dear fellow, you exaggerate things so frightfully! I cannot exactly feel that I am personally responsible for the atrocious deed. It took place by some mysterious dispensation of the will of God."

"In other words, it was a theatrical effect, a dissolving-view, a nursery-tale, 'got up' as an appeal to your better feelings, in the hope of making your life more moral and correct. Now, don't let us have any unreality in the matter. Is sin, or is it not, truly and literally the occasion of Christ's death?"

"Of course it is."

"Then Christ's death is the exact measure of

the guilt of sin; and yet you can sin, and be merry. Nay, there is something more to be said about it than this. Pray, what is the punishment of sin?"

"Hell."

"And hell means everlasting torment in unquenchable fire?"

"Yes, undoubtedly."

"Then sin is not only the measure of the guilt incurred by Christ's death, but it is the measure of the sinner's agony in hell; which agony, you say, is everlasting. And yet you can sin, and be merry. I suppose," continued Curtis, "that you really do believe in hell."

"Certainly I do."

"And you think that most people will go there?"

"Indeed I do not think any thing so dreadful."

"Come now, old fellow, let us have the courage and the honesty to look our difficulties in the face. You have every reason to believe, have you not, from a comparison of scripture and Christian teaching with the general condition of the world, that only a small proportion of mankind will eventually be saved?"

"Yes," I answered, after some little hesitation: "I am afraid that I am bound to think so."

"Then will you kindly explain to me how it comes to pass that you can soberly believe, and eloquently preach, that an overwhelming majority of your fellow-creatures will be burnt alive throughout all eternity in the flames of hell, and yet can find time or inclination at any moment of your life for any other work than the work of rescuing the souls around you from their appalling doom?"

"I never said any thing about being burnt alive. Your way of putting things, my dear friend, is perfectly horrible."

"I wish it to be perfectly horrible. Hell, I presume, is intended to be perfectly horrible. I would speak of it in words a hundred-fold more horrible, if only I knew how. Pray, if the everlasting torment, in unquenchable flames, of an immortal soul, does not mean being burnt alive forever, what does it mean? Moreover, I should imagine that you are not quite certain that you will escape the punishment of hell yourself."

"Ah, no!" said I: "indeed I am not."

"And you can contemplate even so much as the distant possibility of being tortured with agonies insupportable for ages and ages, and millions of ages more, and all the while can laugh and joke, and talk of politics and business and pleasure, as if you were the happiest fellow on this earth!"

"My dear Curtis, I cannot always be thinking about hell. I think of it sometimes, of course; and when I do so the contemplation makes me very sad."

"Very sad! I should think it did. And it is only *sometimes*, I take it, that the majority of your brethren think of it; for I cannot say that they strike me, on the whole, as a particularly *sad*-looking set of men. Now, let us put the matter logically and fairly. This most frightful doctrine of an everlasting fire is literally true, or literally false. There is no intelligible theory between the two extremes. A subject of such gigantic importance refuses to accommodate itself to the dimensions of a commonplace contingency. You parsons do actually stand in imminent peril of being burnt alive forever, or else you do not. The souls committed to your keeping, or a certain proportion of them, are destined to spend a whole eternity in torment, or they are destined to nothing of the kind. If they are so destined, and if you, unless by precept and example you have done all in your power to save them, shall have your part in their unutterable woe, what can you do from morning to night but pray for them, and weep for them, and implore them earnestly to escape at any cost from the horrors of an unquenchable flame? Obviously there is nothing else that you can do; and, if at any instant you put your hands to any other work, nobody to whom you preach will suppose that you really believe in the terrors which you threaten."

"I don't see that at all," answered I. "May not a priest hold his doctrines fast, and yet for a time forget them? Nay, may he not even commit wilful sin, and all the while be fully persuaded that he shall suffer for it at the last?"

"No doubt he may. But I do not happen to be speaking of wilful sin, or weaknesses of the flesh, or inconsistencies of conduct either. Of course, a thoroughly religious man may yield to temptation again and again, and yet may have a clear conviction that God's eye is watching him, and that God's law will bring him to judgment. The Christian priest, no less than the Christian layman, must be continually beset by the allurements of the world. This is another matter altogether. Heathen as I am, I trust that I shall never so far forget myself as to talk to a clerical friend about his private sins. I am talking of your visible, external, premeditated mode of life. My point is this, — that in the face of your alleged persuasion that you yourself and all your flock are standing, for all you know, upon the very brink of an everlasting hell, you have deliberately chosen, and cheerfully maintain, a course of occupations, and a position in society, which no man could possibly endure for half a day, who really believed himself and those dear to him to be placed in any such peril. I do not pretend that you are leading a *godless* life. What I say is, that, if you are not leading a downright *ascetic* life, — the life of Christ, and nothing less, — you waste words upon the air when you preach the punishment of eternal flames."

"It never was intended," I replied, beginning to unwire the cork of another bottle of soda-water, — "it never was intended that I should lead an ascetic life; and I could not do it if I tried."

"Then you must give up your doctrine. No other life has any sense whatever, when a man comes to talk about being burnt alive in an unquenchable fire. Do let us strip these words of their conventional 'unmeaningness,' let us clear away the rust which the traditions of unthinking ages have fastened on them, and let us think what they really signify. To be burnt alive in an unquenchable fire, — it is literally this, and worse than this, or else it is nothing. Whether the fire be spiritual or material, whether the pain be mental or bodily, the idea presented to the mind is always the same. The lost are to dwell forever amid such excruciating torment, that they shall curse the day when they came into the world. Could you, could I, could any one of us, believing it to be, let us only say, uncertain, whether this horrible doom will be our own doom or not, take thought for any conceivable thing besides? What do I care whether I live in a house, or a cellar; whether my business fails, or prospers; whether the world goes on, or collapses altogether? — what are all these things to me, and what are thousands of other such things to me, if this life is to last me for thirty, forty, fifty years, and then, unless all my hours and minutes have been given to God, this very body of mine in which I live and move is to be burnt forevermore? These things could be absolutely nothing to me. At no single instant could I dare to relax my vigilance, lest some unforeseen temptation should insnare me in the toils of hell. The ascetic life might cost me a superhuman struggle; to weep and pray incessantly might seem a hard and cheerless lot: but, if utter prostration of myself before God were the price at which I was to escape being damned, I would pay the price ungrudgingly with the few short years of this paltry life, and take my reward hereafter."

"But, my good fellow, you forget that both you and I have certain duties to perform, with which the ascetic life is incompatible."

"What duties? If they be such duties as will prevent my keeping perpetually before me the dread of hell, I shall decline to attempt them."

"It unfortunately happens," I replied, "to be your special business not only to attempt a variety of secular duties, but satisfactorily to fulfil them; and, what is more, God will call you to account for your negligence if you leave them undone."

"Will he? Then he has bidden me do things contradictory to one another: he has reduced religion to an absurdity, and as such I shall reject it. I cannot serve him, and *not* serve him; think of him, and *not* think of him; remember the penalty of hell, and forget it, in order that I may fix my mind with earnestness on something which merely concerns this lower world. Besides, in a matter of such moment, I choose to be on the safe side. God may or may not have laid upon me some purely secular task; I cannot tell: but I *can* tell, supposing your gospel to be true, that he has threatened me with eternal fire. He will not damn me, because, through fear of his awful judgments, I make my whole life a life of incessant prayer. My destiny for ages and ages to come is of such overwhelming importance to me, that nothing else is worth considering. No plausible suggestions that duty summons me elsewhere, no subtle hints that I have duties to discharge in this or that society, shall turn me a hair's-breadth from the one purpose of my life. Stretched out in the distance before me, I see the everlasting hell; and he who comes to me with whisperings that would divert my gaze towards something else shall be to me a tempter from the Evil One."

"Well," said I, "on some few men of a specially sensitive turn of mind, the fear of hell might possibly operate in the way which you describe. But it is lucky that most persons are not similarly affected: if they were, the world could not go on."

"The old argument back again. I thought we had disposed of that objection long ago. And suppose the world did not go on? Admitting the orthodox belief about heaven and hell, what possible harm could happen to any living soul, if all mankind agreed to leave trade and politics alone, and kneel before God with prayer and weeping till the judgment-day?"

"If mankind agreed to any thing so foolish, mankind would be simply thwarting the express designs of the Almighty. When the Creator made this earth, he meant that its resources should be utilized; and when he made man supreme over his other works, and gave him a quick intelligence and a cunning hand, he meant that these gifts should be employed" —

"To what purpose, may I ask?"

"Indirectly, to the glory of God, but ostensibly and practically, no doubt, to the advancement and prosperity of man."

"I am to gather, then, that man was sent upon this earth in order that he might work out his own advancement and prosperity?"

"I did not say so," answered I. "I should

rather imagine that he was sent on earth to work out the salvation of his soul."

"And upon what theory is it proposed that the attainment of two such very distinct objects should be combined, — that man should work for temporal advancement and spiritual welfare at one and the same time?"

"Upon this very simple theory, which Scripture and common-sense alike suggest as the only theory that can stand. A man must choose an honest calling; must labor diligently in fulfilling its duties; must be temperate in his habits, moderate in his pleasures, and chaste in his behavior; must love his neighbor as himself; must say his prayers night and morning, go to church on Sunday, and do his best to follow the prayers, and profit by the sermon. If he does this, and does it from a good motive, because he knows that he is thereby pleasing God, he will have solved the problem how to combine the attainment of temporal advancement with spiritual welfare; and, when he dies, God will take him to heaven."

"Should he, unhappily, fail in solving this apparently not very difficult problem?"

"Why, in that case," said I, "when he dies, he will go to hell."

"And you positively mean me to accept it as your belief, — the belief of an intellectual, educated man, — that success in the life of which you have just drawn a picture can possibly win heaven, or that failure in such a life can possibly merit hell? My dear fellow, you must perceive at once that both your reward and your punishment are out of all proportion to the amount of service rendered or withheld. The average life of the average exemplary layman, who gives most of his time to business, a fair proportion of it to pleasure, and a decent scrap of it to God, could neither entitle any man to the eternal blessedness of heaven, nor make him fit to appreciate its joys. Such a life might, indeed, be a suitable preparation for some future state of existence, in which loftier flights of commercial enterprise might be attempted, or nobler triumphs of mechanical skill might be achieved; but such a life could never lead up to pleasures in which angels take delight, or discover amid the throng of ransomed saints the haven where it would be."

"You must remember," I observed, "that our ideas of heaven are purely conventional and imaginary. We talk to children about white-robed martyrs singing the praise of God, because such a thought conveys a beautiful and appropriate picture to their childish minds. But it is far more probable that heaven will hereafter prove to be a state of existence wherein our occupations will be something like those of this present life, but purer in their nature, and more exalted in their aim."

"Well," replied Curtis, "if I were asked to choose, I confess that I should be inclined to adopt the childish theory as the more rational of the two. At any rate, if you do not accept the angelic and æsthetic idea of heaven, you must admit that Scripture gives you no other. And, unless Christianity be altogether a delusion, it seems to me that the Bible representation of future blessedness must be received as substantially true. It is the only theory which is in the least degree consistent with the other Christian beliefs. For heaven was purchased by the blood of Christ. His death must be taken as the measure, not only of the sinner's guilt, and of his punishment in hell, but also of the just man's standard of holiness, and of his reward hereafter. It could not have been worth while for Christ to die, that he might win for man grace enough to enable him to serve God and mammon decently in this life, and enjoy at the last a heaven in which it should be his highest happiness to serve God and mammon rather better than before; but it *was* worth while for Christ to die, if, by his death, he might procure for man the power of closely imitating his pure and spotless life, and might thus prepare him, day by day, for fellowship with himself at God's right hand. You tell us in your sermons that Christ is the corner-stone of Christian truth. Let me tell you, in return, that, unless Christ be the corner-stone also of Christian practice, the fabric of your Christianity will tumble down. Accept the fact that his example is literally the model of every Christian's life, and all things concerning Christianity become, I do not say credible, but, at all events, intelligible, and consistent with themselves. Then the precepts of the gospel are no longer unpractical and ridiculous, but hold up a standard which is meant to be attained. Then heaven ceases to be the impossible abode of easy-going, good-natured, respectable members of modern English society, who could not by any means appreciate its joys; and we begin to comprehend how incessant private prayer, and daily public worship, and works of self-denial and mercy, can form the only fitting preparation for a state of blessedness, wherein the vision of God will be man's great reward, and Christ shall shine as the sun forever. Then, also, the mystery unravels itself, how man, by any amount of wickedness, can deserve the fearful punishment of hell. If Christ has given him a model which he may follow if he will, and man deliberately rejects it, laughs at it, and thwarts and hinders those who strive to copy it, with his bitterest malignity and spite; if Christ was put to death by every sin of man, and man persists in sinning still, that he may see Christ crucified afresh, and horribly feast his eyes upon the agony of his God, — then it becomes intelligible to me that the awful penalty of an everlasting fire should alone suffice to expiate the guilt of the unrepentant sinner. But your modern theory of a Christian life and its reward hereafter is more than I can understand. You have thrust away your corner-stone; and the fair fabric of Christianity has become a ruined heap of inconsistencies and absurdities. You discard the example of Christ, because to follow his example would make you ridiculous in the sight of men, — the very thing which he declares that his followers must always be. You thoroughly enjoy all our heathen comforts and amusements; and when we taunt you with your dishonesty, and tell you that you are serving God and mammon, you have the unblushing impudence to look us sanctimoniously in the face, and assure us that we are quite mistaken in supposing that you really take delight in worldly pleasures; that you only indulge in them because you think it a duty, and that your heart is all the while intently fixed on higher and purer joys. You confess that this life is but as a moment in comparison of eternity, and that at every instant of the day you are preparing yourselves either for heaven or hell: and yet you talk as heathen talk, and laugh as heathen laugh, and dine as heathen dine; doing all these things, as I said before, not because the weakness of the flesh has suddenly betrayed you, but because you dare to pretend that God, the Father of the very Christ whom your sins have murdered, sent you into the world in order that you might live very much as other men. The plain fact is, my friend, that you have invented for yourselves a new Christ, and you want a new gospel, and a new heaven and hell, to correspond. And, what is more, you want a new set of prayers and psalms. I don't know whether familiarity has bred contempt, and taught you to look upon your litany and collects as an unmeaning form of words; but I do know this, that your prayer-book, from beginning to end, breathes the spirit of such a true devotion, places the suppliant in a position so touchingly helpless before God, so abject in his dependence upon the grace he seeks through Christ, so deeply contrite for the sins wherewith he has grieved the Holy Spirit, that I, a wicked unbeliever, can scarcely hear it read without being moved to tears. How can one who has said to himself, for example, the Collect for the Sixth Sunday after Epiphany, or for Easter Eve, or the General Thanksgiving, or the fifty-first or hundred and nineteenth psalm, — who has said these, and felt them, and dwelt upon them with any approach towards earnestness of mind, — how such a man can leave the church in perfect good-humor with himself, smiling and cheerful, and light of heart, and talk common worldly talk to common worldly people till it is time to go to service again, is more than a simple heathen can comprehend."

"My dear fellow," I expostulated, "you set up such a ridiculously high standard!"

"I set up a standard? Indeed, I do no such thing. It is Christ, your professed example, who sets up the standard. It is the eternity of possible bliss in heaven that sets up the standard. It is the risk of falling into an everlasting hell that sets up the standard. It is the prayer that you mutter with your own false lips that sets up the standard. It is nothing to me. I don't want you to follow the example of Christ: you would be very stupid company for me if you did. I don't want you to live as if you were trying to win a place in heaven: there would be few points of sympathy between us if you did. I don't want you to talk and act as if you were thinking of your solemn litanies in church: we should see but little of each other if you did. All I say is, in the name of common, decent honesty, be one thing or the other. Be a Christian, or be a heathen. Don't repeat petitions which simply have no sense, except in the mouth of one who is copying Christ in every word and deed; and then turn out into the world, and lead a life a trifle better, or a trifle worse, than that of an intelligent Hindoo. If your prayer-book lessons of holiness are too strict for you, have the candor to confess it, and own that your psalms are out of date, and that your collects were written in days when men regarded Christ's example in a different light from the light which civilization and common-sense have since revealed to you. If a Christian can repeat his confessions and thanksgivings without actually sobbing aloud, it may, at any rate, be fairly expected that he cannot repeat them, and really feel them, without hurrying home after service, and pouring out his burst of penitence alone in his secret chamber before God. Do you think, old fellow, that your good people in a general way have the slightest notion what sort of a life it is to which the words of their own prayer-book pledge them? nay, that they have ever taken the trouble to reflect what their litanies and kyries mean?"

"I hope they have," replied I; "but you forget that a Christian is bidden to do other things besides weep and mourn. St. Paul says that we are to 'rejoice evermore;' and the very psalms of which you speak are full of expressions which are designed to move the heart to gladness, and not to sorrow."

"Yes," he returned; "and here is yet another instance of Scripture perverted and misapplied. The Bible says that the Christian is to rejoice; but how? His joy is to be, from first to last, a purely *spiritual* joy. I defy you to produce a single text which countenances your taking delight in any earthly gratification whatever. Those who choose to have their pleasure now will lose it hereafter. It is, of course, quite easy to conceive, from a Christian point of view, that the man who is daily struggling against his sins, and following the steps of Christ, should be inwardly ten thousand times more happy than the worldly man. On his knees, in close communion with his Lord, the holy and pure of heart may be satisfied with a fulness of joy which the man of pleasure has never known. But apart from Christ, or from matters in which Christ is more or less directly concerned, it is quite impossible that he who is living a Christ-like life should be merry and glad. Even if he could feel happy on his own account, there is the wickedness of many whom he loves, which must needs distress him. Would you believe that my dearest friend upon earth was on trial for his life, and would very probably be hanged, if you met me somewhere at five-o'clock tea, talking nonsense to some young lady? So neither will I believe that you imagine yourself, or any one for whom you care, to stand in danger of everlasting torment, when I see that you are able to dismiss the subject from your thoughts, as if there were no particular cause for alarm. I cannot believe it. Unless you are prepared to maintain that the possibility of damnation forevermore is consistent with a careless, joyous laugh, in short, that the prospect of being burnt alive through countless ages is a cheerful prospect, rather than otherwise, you shall hold me excused if I pronounce my opinion, that, somewhere or other in the relation between faith and practice, there exists among you modern merry-making Christians a gigantic absurdity; and what the absurdity is, any poor benighted heathen with a head on his shoulders must have the wit to see. You are trying to serve God and mammon: you are trying to make things spiritual accommodate themselves pleasantly and inoffensively to things material: you are trying to make Christ hide every characteristic feature of his face, so that he may walk harmless and undisturbed among the haunts of men, winking at their worldliness, adapting his precepts to their common-sense, and never presuming to hurt the feelings, or wound the self-love, of any living soul. This is what you are trying to do; and, in making the attempt, you have involved yourselves in a maze of impossibilities. In support of a position illogical in itself, you are always most illogically arguing backwards."

"What upon earth do you mean by arguing backwards?"

"I will tell you what I mean. You paint an ideal, a very perfect and happy ideal, of a gentleman or a lady; you invest this ideal with all the qualities which go towards forming such characters in life as one delights to meet: and then, because you have been taught to look upon Christ as the highest type of manhood, you call your ideal gentleman a Christian. He is no more like Christ than he is like the stars. As a gentleman, he is forced to do, every day of his life, things which Christ never did; and is forbidden almost to speak one word which Christ ever spoke. If, instead of arguing backwards, painting your ideal first, and then assuming, that, because he is so good, he must be like Christ; if, instead of this, you would argue forwards, would consider what Christ said and did, and make your model Christian say and do the same, —you would very soon perceive that the words "Christian" and "gentleman" are simply contradictory. A gentleman is a man whom it is at any moment a pleasure to meet, because you may be sure that he will set you at your ease, and do or say something to make you happy. A Christian is a man whom it is at all times the greatest nuisance to meet, because you may be perfectly certain, if he be really in earnest, that he will do his best to make you as ill at ease as possible; will remind you incessantly of the flames of hell, and rebuke you to your face, regardless of good manners, for every thing you do or say which savors of this present world. The truth is, as I said before, that you have adopted for yourselves the best and purest form of civilization, and called it Christianity. It is not Christianity at all. Christianity begins just where the best and purest form of civilization leaves off, and sets to work to oppose and thwart its progress at every turn. Civilization permits people to work hard all day that they may become wealthy, to enjoy thoroughly their hours of recreation, and to sit down to a comfortable dinner in the evening. Christianity tells a man that he must give his money to the poor, no matter whether political economists approve or not; frightens him out of his wits, in the midst of his pleasures, by the threat of everlasting fire; and bids him leave the dinner-table as soon as the bare wants of existence are supplied, that he may spend the rest of the evening in prayer for the safety of his soul, rather than in the refreshment of his body. I am not saying that this is what men and women in modern society ought to do. Heaven forbid that any fellow-guests of mine should ever be so eccentric! All I say is, that this is clearly what Christianity enjoins them to do, and that, if they stop short of this, they are civilized heathens."

"Do you soberly mean me to gather from your words, my dear Curtis, that a man cannot be a Christian without making an ass of himself?"

"I do soberly mean you to gather just precisely that very thing. I say emphatically that every true follower of Christ must needs make himself ridiculous in the eyes of worldly people, in the opinion of modern society, every time he speaks or acts."

"But, my dear friend," I expostulated, "you really have no right to force upon a faith so venerable as ours a *reductio ad absurdum*."

"That," answered he, "is no affair of mine. You must get out of any such difficulty as best you may. You parsons volunteer these extraordinary doctrines; and you should be prepared to accept the consequences that ensue. It is a perfect mockery to tell me that I must imitate a Christ, who, all his life, was covered with reproach and ridicule, and in the same breath to tell me that I am not required to expose myself to ridicule and reproach. It is sheer nonsense to threaten me with a hell which is to torture my undying body forevermore, and then to explain that it is by no means intended that I should be terrified continually at the thought of it. This is part of your genuine modern-Christian plan of arguing backwards. You want me to lead a pleasant, gentlemanly life, and then to try and make myself believe that this was the life which Christ led; when the Bible says it was not. You tell me, that, up to the last minute of my existence, I shall be in danger of the everlasting flames of hell; and, when I object that the bare possibility of such a fate leaves me no choice but to weep and groan from morning till night incessantly, you say that I am forcing upon your most holy faith a *reductio ad absurdum*, and that I am a wicked infidel for my pains. Whether there be a hell, or no, may be judged a matter of opinion; but it can be no matter of opinion what sort of life those who stand in peril thereof must lead. All the doctors and fathers and schoolmen that ever lived cannot alter the inexorable law that pain is dreadful, and the pains of hell so unutterably dreadful, that no man can believe in them, and smile. Your Christian doctrines are too tremendous ever to appear trivial. If they are true at all, they are so awfully true as to leave us no room for any thought beside them. Do what you will, you cannot change eternal fire into any thing else but fire eternal. Theologically, no doubt, it would be highly convenient that there should be a hell and no hell, a heaven and no heaven, a Christ and no Christ. But it is only theologically that such fictions can stand: for practical purposes, we must have one thing or the other. If you will only believe it, my friend, there is no middle way between the Christianity of Christ, and downright infidelity. Heaven becomes utter nonsense, unless it was opened to all believers by the sharpness of Christ's death, and unless those alone shall win it, who, through ridicule and insult and shame, have visibly at every moment crucified themselves into fellowship with his sufferings. Hell becomes utter nonsense, unless it is the penalty of sins so horrible, that the Christian ought to spend half his life upon his knees, weeping for his own and his brother's guilt. Your prayer-book becomes utter nonsense, unless the Christian worshipper leaves the house of God with downcast face and tearful eyes, afraid to lose by lightsome gesture the grace that he has received, and bravely resolving that men may scoff and sneer and persecute, but he will clothe his very life and conversation with the words that he has offered up in prayer. Your gospel becomes utter nonsense, unless it is the record of One who came to set his mark forever upon a handful of devoted followers, who in every generation should be known from all others by their likeness to their Lord, who should be hated of all men for his name's sake, who should literally and in every sense renounce this present world, and lay up for themselves a treasure in the world to come. These are the signs by which I should look to distinguish the Christianity of Christ. But I see no such signs in the modern English Christian; and therefore I remain a heathen. By this fourfold test I try you, — by your prayers, your preaching, your hopes, and your fears; and I find your lives wanting at every point. You follow the example of a Christ of whom the gospel does not tell: you utter prayers which commit you to such a life as you do not pretend to lead: you talk of a heaven so little precious in your eyes, that, for the sake of winning it, you cannot give up the paltry joys of earth: you whisper solemnly about a hell whose terrors sit so easily upon your mind, that any trifling pursuit suffices to drive the thought of them far away. This is the personal witness on which a reasonable creature in search of truth is asked to believe in the astounding miracle of the incarnation and death of God. Pardon me, my friend, if I assure you that such testimony will convince no man whose assent is worth obtaining. To take one test only from among the four by which I am trying you, — it is enough to turn a believer into an infidel, to hear one of your average parsons discourse about the punishment of hell. He declares, for instance, that those who do not hate and speedily renounce every kind of sin will be cast into the lake of brimstone. He declares, moreover, that although every one who hears him may, if he pleases, obtain grace enough to enable him to avoid this terrible doom, it is, nevertheless, almost a certainty that only a few, a very, very few, will seek that grace, and use it. Therefore it follows, as a logical consequence, that nine-tenths or three-fourths, or any fair proportion you please to take, of the average Sunday congregation, will suffer excruciating torture forever and forevermore."

"How dare you," I remonstrated, — "how dare you make such cold-blooded calculations? I shudder to hear you use language so fearfully wicked. The Bible, you must know, expressly discourages any speculation as to the number of the lost or saved."

"My dear fellow," answered Curtis, "I do not dare to make any calculations at all. I merely take the general estimate, as I find it laid down in the orthodox sermon. All preachers to whom I have ever listened agree in declaring that only a small minority of mankind will probably be saved. A small minority means, I suppose, about one in ten; but it shall mean nine in ten, if anybody likes that better. The question of a few more or a few less is quite immaterial to my argument. If one man in a congregation, or one man in a parish, or one man in a diocese, is going to be burnt alive for millions upon millions of centuries, I do not quite see how the minister whom God has appointed to rescue his soul can ever sleep at night, or ever contemplate so horrible a destiny without floods of tears. On the average minister, however, this responsibility seems to sit very lightly. He delivers his most awful message; he tells his people plainly that if they sin they will be damned; he knows for certain that they will go on sinning all the same; and under a grave apprehension, not to say a strong impresion, that several of his cherished acquaintances and kindly neighbors will be devoured in flames unquenchable, he walks home to his vicarage, jokes with his wife, romps with his children, chaffs his friend, sits down comfortably to his luncheon, and thoroughly enjoys his slice of cold roast beef, and his glass of bitter beer. Will any man in his senses believe that he means what he has just been saying in his sermon? Of course, he will believe nothing of the sort; and therefore it has come to pass that England is full of intelligent laymen who doubt and disbelieve. How, indeed, should they accept such teaching? The judge, when he sentences a criminal to a mere transient death, speaks with broken voice, and scarcely restrains his tears. The priest, the minister of God, can talk of the intolerable death eternal of souls committed to his charge, and talk of it with placid face, in neatly-rounded phrases, and calm, collected tones. Will any one believe him? Ah, no! He may win applause for his eloquence, but he will not souls. His congregation will watch him home, and see how his own words tell upon his life; and when they find that he can give up his Monday morning to worldly business, and his Tuesday afternoon to worldly pleasure, while the fire, according to his own account, is being already kindled, which may devour the choicest of his flock, they will take his Sunday's sermon for what it is worth, and nothing more. He may please to imagine that he believes in an everlasting hell; but, when next he proclaims his belief, he can hardly be offended if the straightforward Briton should shake his head, and smile."

"Then do you mean to say," I inquired, "that the parson has not a perfect right to his wife, and his luncheon, and his bitter beer?"

"He has every possible right," rejoined Curtis, "as far as I am concerned, to all the good things which his means may enable him to procure. But then, you see, I do not believe in his doctrine. No more does he. He cannot hold it, and care for a single earthly joy. As long as there remains but the suspicion of a chance, that, if he fails in bringing men to Christ, he will be burnt alive forever, so long, if he have ordinary human feelings, will every thought of his heart be given to the one work in hand. He may, at some moment of temptation, forget the doom which threatens him; or he may have altogether failed to realize what everlasting punishment actually means; or he may dismiss the matter from his mind as an incomprehensible mystery, which he is bound to teach, but which he cannot seriously believe. But if he does believe it; if he literally, truly, honestly believes that for millions upon millions of ages, as long as God himself exists, God will torment in hell, with agonies intolerable, an overwhelming majority of the men and women and children now living merrily upon this earth, — if he can believe this, and all the while can eat and drink, and laugh and play, and go to his bed in peace, he must be without exception the most extraordinary person that the great Creator ever made."

"Well," said I, after thinking for a while, "making allowance for your absurdly exaggerated way of putting things, I am bound to acknowledge that your fourfold test of a true religion is theoretically sound. We ought, of course, to imitate Christ, to live as we pray, to cherish the thought of heaven, and to dread hell. One thing, however, which occurs to me is this, — that, if your standard of Christian holiness were generally adopted (I won't distress you by saying that 'the world could not go on,' but), the species could not be propagated. Art, science, literature, and every legitimate occupation of man, would have to be sacrificed at once; and the great human family itself would speedily disappear."

"If it be so," replied my friend, "even then, unless you can show where my argument breaks down, I shall but have made it the more apparent that your religion is a superstition and an absurdity. But, supposing myself to be a Christian, I should strongly hesitate to admit your position, that the truest type of a Christ-like life need interfere with matrimony, or with art and science in their devotional application. The instinct which leads man to seek a wife must be just as divine in its appointment as that which teaches him to eat when he is hungry, or sleep when he is tired; and the chaste husband has positively nothing more in common with the man of unclean life than he who has partaken sparingly of the simplest food has with the drunkard who is being disgracefully carried home. Besides, I can readily conceive how the bringing-up of children in the fear of God, and the fashioning of a household after a strictly scriptural model, should beget a daily succession of duties eminently Christian. It is difficult, perhaps, to concede that matrimony is equally open to the priest, simply because one does not understand how he can possibly find time for even the preliminary steps which such a state entails. Think, for example, what mischief the Devil might do in the parish, while the parson was making love to the squire's daughter. But for priest and layman alike there must be a variety of secular pursuits available, wherein the mind of each might find its needful refreshment, and whereby the glory of God might be directly and visibly promoted. In the first place, there is natural history. Considering that the great and wise Creator, as you gentlemen profess to believe, has made in England alone something like ten thousand species of insects, and more than seventeen hundred wild flowers, — to say nothing of sea-weeds, snails, funguses, and creatures of divers kinds innumerable, — it is not much to your credit that scarcely one so-called Christian in a thousand should know a moth from a butterfly, a beetle from a cockroach, or a hawkweed from a dandelion. Then there is architecture, music, painting, poetry, every one of which, as your churches and cathedrals testify, may be consecrated to the service of God. The Primate of all England is said to have expressed an opinion, in his recent charge, that the musical portion of your cathedral services is 'overdone.' It has been very much the reverse of 'overdone,' in any case within my own observation. Among much that was extremely beautiful, I have generally chanced to hear your noble aisles and transepts desecrated with a composition which was about as worthy of performance in a Gothic choir as the daubings of some village sign-painter would be worthy of a place in the National Gallery; and which was performed after a fashion such as any educated audience in a concert-room would have saluted with hisses and groans. In fact, a comparison of your cathedrals with the music celebrated therein provokes a somewhat instructive contrast between the Christianity of your forefathers and the heathenism of yourselves. You have abandoned that extravagance of Christian love which lavished decoration ungrudgingly on roof and arch and pillar, that God might have the best of every thing, whether any practical end were served, or not; and you have adopted the calculating rule of genuine heathen economy, by which every occupation in which man is not earning either money or temporal enjoyment is very properly regarded as a simple waste of time, is reduced to the scantiest dimensions possible, and is rendered with the minimum of cost and the minimum of labor. Unless your glorious relics of ecclesiastical art are to testify to the pious superstition of your ancestors, but to nothing more, there surely must be scope, beneath the shadow of their walls, for the development of many a hallowed taste, the dedication of many a precious gift, and the employment of many a half-hour spared from the day's routine of bread-winning, and sacrificed to God. I am glad," continued Curtis, "that our subject has led us to speak of cathedrals; because I can soberly declare that nothing which I see around me tends so constantly to confirm my view of the barefaced heathenism of modern Christianity as the attitude which you nineteenth-century churchmen have assumed towards these monuments of ancient piety. You possess an inheritance of noble structures, which, on your present principles, it would be considered a wanton misuse of capital to build; and you perform therein a service meagre, miserable, and mean, every accent of which gives the palpable lie to your claim of fellowship with the Christian architect of old. You will never persuade us infidels that you believe in God, until every Christian among you, moved by decent gratitude for benefits received, kneels twice every day in his cathedral or his parish church, and there, with voice, with alms, or with whatever talent God has bestowed upon him, bears his part in offering the most faultlessly beautiful act of worship which Christian art can devise."

"My dear fellow," said I, "people nowadays have something else to do. We are practical men; and we simply have not time to go to church every day, and offer up such a service as you propose."

"Was Christ a practical man?" asked Curtis in return; "or was he one who outraged every worldly maxim, and set common-sense at defiance every time he spoke? Ah, my friend! how is it that you will not have the honesty to confess that Christ has grown old-fashioned in your eyes, and that you have become a heathen for the purpose of enjoying more comfortably this present life, retaining in the background a mere sentiment of Christ, to help you to look forward with complacency to the life eternal? It is your dishonesty, and not your dogmatizing, which has lost for you your influence over the hearts of men. You might teach a hundred Athanasian Creeds, with a hundred damnatory clauses added on to each, if only you lived and moved as men who believed such dogmas to be true. But you must not cling fast to Christ when you want to claim unity with him in doctrine, and break away from him, as if he were out of date, when you want to be merry like other men. They tell me that your bishops are likely soon to meet in conference, for the purpose of deciding what concessions shall be made to the public as regards the Athanasian Creed. They may save themselves the trouble. The public don't want any concessions in any matter so totally beside the point at issue. When your creeds have been mangled and mutilated till no ancient council would recognize them, your psalms and collects will still remain, to set the layman wondering what upon earth you mean; and every sentence of your gospel will ring out its mocking comment on the average priest's or bishop's life, as a damnatory clause. What all men everywhere demand, and what you parsons obstinately refuse to grant, is a plain answer to the very plainest question that mortal lips have ever framed. We want to know whether the Christianity of the New Testament is false or true; whether Christ was a great philosopher, who taught men noble principles of action, and showed them how to be happier and healthier in this present world; or whether he is the very and eternal God, who took upon him human flesh that we might know for certain how human creatures ought to live; who died on the cross to win for us the power to imitate his brave contempt for earthly dignities and joys; who watches us at this moment from his throne in heaven, to see whether we cling to him, as his disciples clung, through insult and suffering and shame, or deny him by following the fashions of a world which condemned its Lord to die. Tell us, in simple, straightforward words, which of these things Christianity is (it cannot be both of them), which of these things Christ is (he cannot be both of them); and we shall know what sort of value to set upon your threats of everlasting fire. But it is too soon to talk to us of being burnt alive for a whole eternity, when you have not yet succeeded in convincing us, by any special solemnity in your life, or any tokens of holy dread, as you move in and out among us, that you yourselves are altogether satisfied of the reality of Christ's life and death, of the necessity of copying his example, of the unspeakable blessedness of heaven, or the avenging flames of hell. You see, old fellow, there is, unfortunately, so very much about your religion which looks shuffling and unreal! Your miracles won't 'come off,' except on condition that no very scientific witnesses are standing by. Your God is said to be a spirit, because such a description affords a convenient way of accounting for the somewhat suspicious circumstance that no mortal creature has ever seen him. Your heaven is a place for which only one sort of life can possibly be a preparation; and this life you do not lead. Your hell is the scene of tortures so terrific that no human being can contemplate them without turning pale; and you don't seem one bit afraid to run the risk of being sent there. Now, all these things bear the manifest stamp of unreality; and unreality is repulsive to the mind of every honest man. When you talk to the clear-headed Briton of such a religion as this, you can only expect, as Mr. Leslie Stephen says so happily, with reference to another subject, somewhere in 'The Alpine Journal,'—you can only expect that your intelligent listener will 'put the tongue of incredulity into the cheek of derision.' Well may you say that infidelity is making rapid strides. Its strides will become more rapid still. As civilization advances, so does Christianity appear more and more absurd. Fifty years hence, your grandsons will laugh at your simplicity, just as you laugh now at the worshippers of the great goddess Diana. Your parsons will have turned their hands to some more honest trade; and your churches will begin to serve a more practical purpose, as museums of science and art. Reasonable beings will have grown ashamed of an idle and foolish superstition, which bribes men with the promise of impossible delights, and frightens them with the threat of impossible horrors, just as the silly nursemaid frightens your child with stories about Bogy coming round the corner to gobble him up."

"I am sadly afraid," said I, trying to look severe, "that I shall have to give you up, as a hardened infidel."

"Indeed you will," was the reply, "unless you are prepared to favor me with proofs which are decently substantial. Let me see Christians imitating Christ, — imitating not a Christ whom I could fashion for myself out of materials purely heathen, not a Christ whom society accepts already as the pattern philosopher, the embodiment of common-sense, the ideal man, but a Christ who at every point is making himself an intolerable offence to the un-Christlike, a thorn and a scourge to every man who does not lie stretched at the foot of his cross, weeping over the sins which nailed him there, loving him with a love which all the world can see, and fearing only lest he should sharpen the agony of his Saviour's death by one unkind or unholy word. Show me a Christian who is imitating visibly such a Christ as this, and I will show you a heathen (heathen not out of stubborn choice, but heathen because there is no evidence before him yet to make him any thing better), — I will show you a heathen who will confess that this marvellous tale of Christ and heaven has become credible to him at last, now that the marvellous witness he has looked for is forthcoming; for then it will be possible for me logically to understand how God has left off working miracles, not because the newspaper reporter is looking on, and will publish the proceedings in to-morrow's 'Times,' but because he has made the life and conversation of his chosen ones an ever-present miracle in the sight of men, — because he has given his priests the superhuman courage to defy public opinion, to endure hatred, ridicule, and scorn, to oppose, obstruct, and harass every creed and custom of society, with the very same uncompromising faithfulness wherewith their Master opposed it, when he provoked and exasperated the Jews, till they murdered him out of very spite and fury. I know for certain how Christ would be treated if he were here. I can see the press deriding him, the fine lady picking her way past him in the street, the poor flocking round him as a friend, the magistrate committing him to prison. Let me see his witnesses treated thus, and I will believe that he has sent them. Their Christ-like life in the face of cold modern refinement, in the teeth of cruel common-sense, shall be to me a miracle no less stupendous than the feeding of five thousand in the wilderness, or the raising of Lazarus from the dead. But while I see them claiming the right to live as other men, glorying in the fact that they have no peculiarities, smiling politely on sin, and caressed by those who would have spat upon their Lord, — so long as I see them thus, they shall teach me, if they please, the principles of Christ's philosophy; but they shall not dare to tell me that they are priests of a crucified Christ."

"Well," said I, "I think I can produce a man whose life pretty well fulfils the conditions you lay down; but then, poor fellow, he is as mad as a hatter."

"What is his name? and what special signs of insanity does he display?"

"He is a parson of the name of Ainslie. He came into a lot of money some years ago, with which he built a magnificent church in a wretchedly poor district cut off from my parish. He still has a very large income; but he lives on about two pounds a week, and gives all the rest away. He scarcely eats or drinks or sleeps, and does not very often speak, unless you say something to 'fetch' him; and then, by Jove! he *does* speak, and to some purpose too. When he first came here, he went a good deal into society; but he used to say such very strange things at dinner, that people were constantly getting up, and leaving the room. He never dines out now; and there is not a gentleman in the town who would not punch his head if he met him at his hall-door. The poor people like him tremendously: he is as gentle as a lamb with *them;* but the sight of a decently dressed man or woman in a carriage seems to drive him perfectly insane. Poor fellow! I am very sorry for him. He is awfully nice in so many ways! and, if he would only hold his tongue, he would be the most popular man in ——. Such a generous fellow too! It was only yesterday that I found out something accidentally about him, which I don't think anybody else knows. Some Dissenting minister, who is editor of a low radical newspaper in the town, wrote a lot of scurrilous articles, not long ago, accusing Ainslie of crimes and follies which neither he nor anybody else ever dreamed of committing. Of course, Ainslie took no notice of the thing whatever; in fact, he never knew, until quite lately, that any thing of the sort had been written; and the editor, encouraged by his forbearance, and thirsting for popularity among the roughs, proceeded further to attack the private character of Lord Hungerford, our great conservative peer. Lord Hungerford communicated with his lawyer, and the lawyer communicated with the editor; and the end of it was, that the gentleman of the press was condemned in costs to an enormous amount, and must inevitably have been locked up in jail, had not an anonymous donation been put into his solicitor's hands, which covered all his liabilities, and set him straight again. The reverend editor flatters himself, to this day, that the gift was bestowed by some admiring friend in his congregation; but I happen to know, and I mean some day to inform my radical parishioner, that Ainslie himself was the giver."

"I tell you what," cried Curtis, starting up, "I should like to know that fellow. Could you take me to him?"

"H'm," said I, looking at my watch; "one could hardly go and knock a man up at a quarter past eleven. And yet I don't know. Ten to one we shall find him in his chancel, where he spends pretty nearly half the day and night, praying. We will go now, if you like. There is a lovely moon; and the church is not above half a mile from here."

The half-mile being accomplished, we found the chancel-door unlocked, and the beautiful choir and richly-clothed altar lit up with more than daylight splendor by the tranquil glory of the moon. I recollect its occurring to me, as I closed the door, that this was the way in which I would put it, if ever I wanted to describe a midnight visit to a church. Against the south wall knelt Ainslie, his hands at one time clasped together, at another time clutching at the pillars of the sedilia, and his body moving restlessly about, as if in pain. He was evidently lost in the fervor of his prayer; and we made so little noise, that he did not hear us enter. His words were murmured rather than spoken; and his voice and gestures had clearly escaped beyond control. For a few seconds he would kneel in perfect stillness, till the sorrow which he seemed to have been nursing the while burst out in a passionate sob, and the man appeared to be struggling with himself for some tremendous mastery, or crushing to utter extinction some unwelcome thought that haunted him. At such a time his cry for help rang piteously through the silent night, as he half sighed, half shouted, the long, wailing whisper of his trouble; and at such a time it was that Curtis and myself, unwilling to stop and listen, but more unwilling to retreat, gathered up, and stored in our memories for many and many a day, the fragments of his prayer.

I will not venture to transcribe it: indeed, the words were far too sacred to be written here. But the point which struck me so forcibly, in Ainslie's language no less than in his tone, was this: the way in which the man had somehow got himself into the visible presence of Christ, till he made you feel that he was literally following his Master about through every incident of the past day, and bringing all his actions, one by one, before his great Example, to see how far and whereabouts he had failed.

It became evident to me, in spite of any thing which my natural sense declared to the contrary, that the Christ to whom he prayed was at this moment every whit as close to him as he had ever been to St. Peter or St. John. He laid hold of him, he appealed to him, he caught at his hand for help, he looked up wistfully for his smile, he shrank away like a frightened child from his tenderest reproach. Christ was there, — nobody could doubt it, — there, in that very chancel, holding communion with that prostrate form. Christ was there: and, as for me, I knew that I was outside the circle wherein he could be seen and felt; that I was one of those who thronged and pressed, but could not get nigh to touch; nay, I told myself, in sober earnest, that I was a very scribe or a Pharisee, looking superciliously on. How many a long day and night must this poor fellow have spent upon his knees, before he could have learned how to bring Christ as near as this! How must his whole life have become one unceasing prayer! How must his very breath, as it came and went, have been drinking down deep draughts of grace, and sighing up to Heaven for more! I could not help wondering whether many of our bishops or deans or canons or influential country rectors, the apostles of the modern English Church, were thus engaged at this particular time, or were likely to be found similarly occupied at any time whatsoever; and my mind unconsciously ran back to glimpses of comfortable libraries and snug arm-chairs, for which the portly figure of the occupant had almost been measured with tape and line. I thought of the pleasant hours that one might spend in such a room, "administering" a diocese, or "organizing" parochial work, while the curate or the Sister of Mercy went pottering about the lanes. I pictured to myself the hour of luncheon, and the well-dressed wife and daughters, and the substantial meal; and I fancied that I saw the master of the house look rather cross because the kidneys were not devilled half enough, and because the minced veal, which the cook knew perfectly well was the only other dish that he could touch in the middle of the day, had been pretty nearly poisoned with too much lemon. Then I heard the plans for the afternoon discussed, — which of the party would ride, and which would drive, and what were the visits that ought to be paid; while some of the younger ladies ventured to speculate about the dinner-party in the evening, whether it would go off well. This carried me down to seven or eight o'clock, when the host would courteously entertain his friends, and his friends would drink his wine, and praise it, discoursing about it eagerly, affectionately, as if it were a subject dear to their inmost soul. And thus I travelled back into the drawing-room, where all was blaze and brilliancy, and women smiled and sparkled, each one holding her court as a radiant queen, to whom men paid pretty little acts of homage, and simpered pretty little unmeaning words. All this came rapidly before me; and I could not but contrast a day and night so spent with the days and nights of my poor mad friend kneeling in the moonlight; and I wondered what Christ would have thought of it all, and whether he would have been most at home with Ainslie, in his isolation from the world, or with my hospitable dignitary, whose liberal table was so good for trade, and whose genial habits did so much to cement a happy union between the clergy and the laity. The contrast forced itself upon me; but I would not permit myself to draw an inference which I felt to be unkind. The social life of the average dignitary could not, I felt sure, be altogether a mistake. In so many ways, by private acts of friendship and in public ministrations, such men had won my cordial affection and esteem; and it was quite impossible to contemplate them as indulging one single gratification which Christ would not approve. Ainslie must, unquestionably, be wrong; and I gladly took refuge in my old belief that the poor fellow was morbid or melancholy mad.

These thoughts were still chasing one another through my mind, and I had scarcely formed my last conclusion, when Curtis also began to demonstrate very perceptible signs of being moved as deeply as myself by Ainslie's exceeding earnestness.

"Look here, old fellow," he whispered, in a

broken voice; "I positively cannot stand any more of that, you know. Let us come away home."

Ainslie, however, was by this time aroused; and we two had hardly escaped through the chancel-door, when he joined us in the church-yard. Having explained and apologized for our intrusion, I introduced him to Curtis; and we then learned that he was waiting up to visit, for the third time that day, a parishioner of notoriously evil life, who had been struck down suddenly with scarlet-fever, and was expected to die.

"The doctor has sent me away twice," said Ainslie; "but he promised that I should go again somewhere about this time, if every thing went on well; and he is going to send a boy to fetch me."

"Have you had the scarlet-fever yourself, may I ask?" said Curtis.

"Never," was the reply.

"Then I almost wonder that you are not afraid to go."

"My life, sir," answered Ainslie, "is not

mine, that I should give it, or spare it, as may please me best. It is little enough that I have ever done for Christ; and, if I can serve him better in my death than in my life, I can wish nothing happier for myself than that I may die."

At this moment the youth whom Ainslie was expecting appeared upon the scene, and carried him off to the sick man's chamber. He wished us both a cordial good-night, and started off on his mission with the air of a man who had a great work to do, and meant to do it.

"There is a *reality* about that fellow," observed Curtis, as we were walking home, "which upsets me altogether. I never saw any thing like it before."

"Yes," answered I: "his character has so many good points, that one cannot help feeling for him. It's a thousand pities that he is so frightfully mad."

"Ah!" said Curtis: "they said something like that about Christ, didn't they? — and about St. Paul, and all the rest of them. Mad? Yes, he certainly must be mad. Mad means different from everybody else; and, if Christ were now on earth, he would be so totally different from you modern English Christians, that you would most infallibly put him into an asylum."

During the next few days my friend and I abandoned ourselves entirely to autumn manœuvres, and became too deeply engrossed in the tactics of Northern and Southern armies to talk much about civilization and Christianity. When the March Past was over, and we south-country rustics had seen such a sight on our Wiltshire downs as we shall never see again, I drove Curtis back to my quiet little parsonage-house, and busied myself with a sermon on the evidences, wherewith I hoped to convert him from the error of his ways, on the ensuing Sunday.

I had just concluded an argument so unanswerable that it must needs convince, I felt sure, the very stubbornest heathen, when an ancient matron, who kept house for my friend Ainslie, was shown into the room. Her master, she said, had been "took" with the fever. He *would* go, though warned of the consequences, so he would. It must always be a comfort to her that she had done her duty by him, so it must. But gentlemen were so hard to manage, that she did not know how ever they could expect to keep their health, no more she didn't. From all which I gathered that I really was wanted at my poor friend's house; and, indeed, on my arrival at his bedside, I found that I was not a minute too early. Curtis, rather to my surprise, was already there; and, from certain indications in his face and manner, I could not doubt that some specially earnest conversation had passed between the two.

"I have been telling him," said Ainslie, in a faint and gasping voice, laying his hand on Curtis's arm, "I have been telling him how right he is. It is Christ, Christ only, Christ entirely, Christ as he lived and as he died; not Christ as we modern cowards have dressed him up, so that he may look like other men. It is Christ, or else it is nothing. We are literally copying his life, or else we are civilized, gentlemanly heathens. For Christian truth has all the elements of a profound absurdity, excepting just this one only element, that it is *real.* Take away its reality, and it becomes ridiculous and impossible. Our mysteries are fables, unless we mean them: our God is a myth, unless we show him visibly to men. We cannot hold our own against the clever sceptic, because we have let go Christ; and Christianity without Christ is, of all philosophies, the most unphilosophical. Ridiculous, indeed, to the mind of the natural man our faith must always be, and must have been intended to be, for it belongs to another world than the world in which he moves; but, unless we live out our profession in downright earnest, we make it ridiculous also to him who would fain believe. Our theory of a Creator is ridiculous, our history is ridiculous, our miracles are ridiculous, our heaven and hell are the most ridiculous of all. In this only are we better than ridiculous, — that, at the very least, we are not ashamed to abide by our own absurdities; that we are brave enough not to flinch from the logical issues of our creed; that we have, at any rate, sufficient sense to see, that, if our choice is to lie between things temporal and things eternal, no charter of Christian privilege yet conveyed to us can, by any possibility, give us the right to choose them both together. Times are not changed: it is a device of the Evil One to teach men so. Christ is as he was: his disciples are as they were. He can no more walk about our streets without insult and cruel mockings now than he could walk scathless about Jerusalem in days of old. As men treated him in the year 33, so do they treat him in 1872, and so will they treat him also in thirty-three times 1872. He is Christ; and good-natured, worldly men and women hate him. Let the Christian priest take this as the gauge of his faithfulness, — that good-natured, worldly men and women hate *him* too. Oh, if they should love him, and flatter him, and welcome him at their godless feasts, and make him free of their heathen pleasures, how will he face that day, when his Lord shall search him through and through, and look for the marks of scourge and rod, but look in vain; and feel for the long furrows that the ploughers should have ploughed upon his back, but find no furrows there? . . .

O Thou who hast borne with me so tenderly all these years, and now wilt take to thyself the life wherein I have given thee back so little of thy love! accept, as my last poor offering of gratitude, the thanks I render thee for this great and exceeding mercy; that, as I have followed — ah, so imperfectly! — thy blessed steps, thou hast ever walked before me, not as a *new* Christ, grown dainty and refined, to suit the civilization of the age, but as the selfsame Christ of whom the gospel tells me, — poor, and persecuted, and laughed to scorn."

Three weeks have passed since the foregoing pages were written; and my friend Curtis has returned to London, to resume his practice at the bar. We stood together at dear Ainslie's grave, till the last notes of the resurrection service had died away, and the choristers had come up by turns to cast in their parting gift of flowers, and take a long farewell of one whose like they will never see again. Poor boys! it was as much as they could do to keep their voices steady, as they sang the anthems and psalms; and more than once I feared that they would utterly break down. But I think even their unaffected childish sorrow touched me less than the strong flood of tears which kept on bursting again and again from sturdy men and women who stood and wept on every side. Not only was the churchyard crammed to overflowing, but the street itself would scarcely hold the crowd of mourners. They who had misrepresented him, calumniated him, ground their teeth at him for the pure example that he shed, now stood apart, and brushed off the great drops that started from their eyes, lest their weakness and their self-upbraiding should be seen. Ah! "We fools accounted his life madness, and his end to be without honor. How is he numbered among the children of God! and his lot is among the saints."

Three weeks have passed; and I have just come back from a visit to the grave, over which I have got into the habit of liking to offer up a daily prayer that my death may be as full of hope as his, and my life — well, I have got into the habit, I am afraid, of *not* liking to think much about my life, since the day when I stood with Curtis in the chancel-doorway, and listened to our dear friend's prayer. When I had left a poor handful of late autumn-flowers upon the mound, I looked in at the open door by which we had entered on that memorable night, and started with surprise to see a figure kneeling just where Ainslie had knelt, weeping just as he had wept, and swinging itself to and fro with deep and passionate emotion. There could be no question who it was. A travelling-bag and a coat and umbrella lay close by on the pavement; and I guessed at once that Curtis had suddenly formed the idea of paying me a second visit, that he had just walked from the station, and was recalling his memories of Ainslie by the way. I did not choose to disturb him at that particular moment: so I crept out of sight and hearing, and left him kneeling still.

Whether my friend was simply moved by the very true sorrow with which he mourned dear Ainslie's loss, or whether in that pure life and saintly death he has discovered the witness which he sought, and has become a Christian, I shall probably learn from his own lips this evening. Of this much, however, I feel well assured, — that whatever step such a man may ultimately take will be taken in thorough earnestness of purpose; and that, if he should indeed resolve to offer himself to Christ, he will love him with all his heart and soul.

For myself, I walked slowly and sadly home, feeling more and more dissatisfied with my own position, and becoming at every moment more and more persuaded that this modern Christianity of ours is neither better nor worse than heathenism, civilized and refined; that our God is to most of us the same mere abstract divinity, the same imaginary personification of good, as the gods of classical mythology to the Roman or the Greek; that it is not one whit more possible to serve two masters now, than when the great truth first was spoken, eighteen centuries ago; and that there is absolutely no middle course left open, to any reasonable man, between the literal, untiring imitation of Christ, in life and death, and the downright refusal to believe that he either lived or died.

Supernatural beliefs, I went on to think, do undoubtedly demand supernatural lives; and, if it is not worth our while to live the one, it is utterly foolish to profess the other. At any rate, we have no right to brand the average worldly-minded man as an unbeliever, and threaten him from the pulpit with intolerable agonies in hell, when we meėt him every day on equal terms, and eat his dinner, and drink his wine, and should think it very bad taste to rebuke his worldliness to his face, and very chicken-hearted to burst into tears at the thought of his dreadful doom. We have no right to appropriate a host of Pagan virtues, as if they belonged exclusively to ourselves; as if "heathen" were synonymous with "cannibal," and no one but a Christian could possibly be generous, or considerate, or kind. All these years we have been preaching the gospel of unreality to the world; and the world seems as far from conversion as ever. Is it not rational to suppose that our efforts to make people good and happy might be more successful, if we lived visibly before society as men to whom this earth is absolutely nothing, and the day of judgment is the only matter worth a moment's thought; or else admitted honestly that our standard has hitherto been too high, that we have exaggerated our knowledge of the hereafter, that Christ is but the idol of a popular superstition, and that it is enough for men to live soberly and peaceably in this present world?

www.ingramcontent.com/pod-product-compliance
Lightning Source LLC
LaVergne TN
LVHW021401110826
845150LV00007B/1739

* 9 7 8 1 4 2 5 5 1 3 0 1 6 *